Can Workers Manage?

Post-Bullock essays in the economics of the inter-relationships between ownership, control and risk-taking in industry, with special reference to participation by employees

BRIAN CHIPLIN
*Lecturer in Industrial Economics,
University of Nottingham*

and

JOHN COYNE
*Lecturer in Labour Economics and Industrial Relations,
University of Nottingham*

LJUBO SIRC
*Lecturer in International Economics,
University of Glasgow*

J. B. WOOD   RALPH HARRIS

Published by
THE INSTITUTE OF ECONOMIC AFFAIRS
1977

First published November 1977

© THE INSTITUTE OF ECONOMIC AFFAIRS 1977

ISSN 0073-2818
ISBN 0-255 36103-3

Printed in England by
GORON PRO-PRINT CO LTD,
6 Marlborough Road, Churchill Industrial Estate, Lancing, Sussex

Text set in 'Monotype' Baskerville

CONTENTS

[3]

[4]

[5]

PREFACE

The *Hobart Papers* are intended to contribute a stream of authoritative, independent and lucid analysis to the understanding and application of economics to private and government activity. Their characteristic theme has been the optimum use of scarce resources and the extent to which it can best be achieved in markets within an appropriate framework of laws and institutions or, where markets cannot work or have disproportionate defects, by better methods with relative advantages or less decisive defects. Since the alternative to the market is in practice the state and both are imperfect, the choice between them is essentially made on the judgement of 'market failure' or 'government failure'.

The characteristic unit of production in a market economy is what economists call the firm, as in Professor R. H. Coase's classic article[1] which defined the firm as the area of activity within which the economies of internal organisation exceeded the economies of market relationships with other firms. The most common legal name is the 'company' (although, of course, there are other legal forms, such as partnership and sole traders), and in political economy the 'enterprise'. The optimal direction of the firm, company or enterprise has long been a central pre-occupation of economists. The essence is the risk-taking function of the 'entrepreneur' who assembles capital and labour in his efforts to meet the wants of the consumer in the market. The optimum size of the firm was discussed in a well-established analysis by Professor Sir Austin Robinson[2] in which he analysed the five criteria of technique, management, finance, marketing and risk.

Later economists have discussed the 'maximand' of the firm—the entity or element it tried to maximise—and whether it was the surplus after costs known as 'profit', or turnover, sales, or other less tangible qualities like power or prestige.

Underlying these discussions has been the unavoidable truth that the firm must be owned by someone or other who takes the risk of losing his property or assets if they are not used efficiently in anticipating the products the consumer will demand. Generally the view has been that the assets are best

[1] 'The Nature of the Firm', *Economica*, 1937.

[2] *The Structure of Competitive Industry*, Cambridge University Press, 1931.

[7]

owned by the shareholders who enjoy the prospect of gain but take the risk of loss. There have always been observers who argued that others apart from the shareholders, especially the employees, run the risk of losing their livelihoods if the firm makes wrong decisions and therefore that the employees should be given a say, varying from being informed after the event, to being consulted before the event, to having a voice in decisions themselves. The logic of this view is that others apart from the firm's shareholders and employees—shareholders and employees in other firms that provide supplies or buy its finished products—also run the risk of losing income if the firm makes wrong decisions, and that therefore they too should have a voice in the conduct of the firms to which they sell or from which they buy. This process could be extended until all shareholders, employees, suppliers and purchasers had voices in all firms. Yet this approach overlooks the reality that, in making their decisions in the long-term interests of shareholders, directors take a long-term view of these internal and external groups.

The most recent argument for 'industrial democracy' in Britain is that employees should not be regarded merely as 'hands' who are hired and fired but as people with a continuing interest in the firms that employ them. This view led to the establishment of the Industrial Democracy Committee under Lord Bullock which reached conclusions that could radically derange the structure of firms in British industry. Hobart Paper 77 analyses the economic implications not only of the Bullock proposal, which has been roundly criticised and widely rejected, but also more generally the optimum combination of ownership, control, decision-making, and risk-taking in the conduct of the firm.

Messrs Brian Chiplin and John Coyne of the University of Nottingham set the stage with a discussion of the nature of property rights. They argue that it has been the loosening of the link between ownership and control that has debilitated British industry and that it is desirable to rebuild the link rather than weaken it. Dr Ljubo Sirc uses the system of self-management in Yugoslavia, sometimes referred to as the exemplar of industrial democracy, to go further into the economic repercussions of employee control, in particular on the division of the revenue of the enterprise between current income and investment in capital equipment. In two shorter

[8]

contributions, Mr John Wood discusses the economic implications against the background of the German development of workers' consultation, and Mr Ralph Harris discusses the general conflict of interest between producers and consumers in the conduct of individual firms and industrial policy in general and points to the scope for collusion between employers and employees against the consumer.

Here, as elsewhere, what will emerge from government will probably be proposals that reflect the realities of what economists have been analysing as 'the economics of politics'[1] as well as, or perhaps rather than, the economics of industry and the requirements of the optimum conduct of the firm.

The market economy allows firms to be run by any individual or group that can assemble the capital required to equip it and pay its employees. They can be shareholders, employees, suppliers or customers; and among employees they can be managers, executives, office staff or work-bench operatives: marketing men, accountants, secretaries, technicians, van drivers, or charladies. The only requirement within the firm is that they who own the capital ultimately take the risks. And the requirement outside the firm, essential for the efficient use of resources in the economy as a whole, is that whoever owns and runs the firm shall submit to the requirements of the consumer in the market. If not, the individual firm will not last long, unless it receives artificial respiration by government subsidy, and the economy will not last long before it seizes up in a general collapse of firms. This requirement was well understood by Mr Peter Jay who, in a Wincott lecture,[2] envisaged 'employee sovereignty' provided it rested on a substructure of 'consumer sovereignty'.

The Institute's constitution requires it to dissociate its Trustees, Directors and Advisers from the analysis and recommendations of its authors. Mr Harris and Mr Wood wrote their contributions in their personal capacities. But the Institute presents this *Paper* as an assembly of analyses that confronts issues which face policy-makers and opinion-formers not always ready to accept the consequences of their thinking. It should therefore be of especial interest to teachers and students of

[1] Professor Gordon Tullock, *The Vote Motive*, Hobart Paperback 9, IEA, 1976.

[2] *A General Hypothesis of Employment, Inflation and Politics*, Occasional Paper 46, IEA, 1976.

economics as an attempt to reveal the economic consequences of policies that may be adopted on grounds of political expediency.

July 1977   ARTHUR SELDON

THE AUTHORS

BRIAN CHIPLIN was born in 1945 and educated at King Edward VI Grammar School, Southampton and Nottingham University, where he took first-class honours in industrial economics in 1966. During 1966-67 he was Viyella Research Fellow in the Department of Industrial Economics, University of Nottingham. He has been a lecturer in that department since 1967. His publications include: (with P. J. Sloane) *Sex Discrimination in the Labour Market* (Macmillan, 1976); (with D. S. Lees) *Acquisitions and Mergers: Government Policy in Europe* (Wilton House/*Financial Times*, 1975); and papers in the *American Economic Review, Economic Journal, British Journal of Industrial Relations*.

JOHN COYNE was born in 1951 and educated at Barnsley Holgate Grammar School and Nottingham University where he took first-class honours in industrial economics in 1973. He then undertook two years post-graduate work in the same department before being appointed lecturer in labour economics and industrial relations. His publications include: 'Kinked Supply Curves in the Labour Market', *Journal of Economic Studies*, November 1975.

LJUBO SIRC was born in Yugoslavia in 1920. During the war, he participated in the resistance but also graduated in economics from the University of Ljubljana in 1943. He escaped to Switzerland to report on occupied Yugoslavia and joined Tito's army of liberation in Southern Italy by a roundabout journey through France. He was arrested in 1947 by the Yugoslav government for conspiracy against the State, and imprisoned.

He escaped to Italy in 1955 and made his way to Britain, where he worked as a BBC monitor. In 1960 he took a degree in economics at Fribourg University in Switzerland and thereafter spent a year lecturing at the University of Dacca, East Bengal. Since 1962 he has been a university lecturer in international economics, first at the University of St Andrews, and, since 1965, at the University of Glasgow. His publications include: *Outline of International Trade* and *Outline of International Finance*, Weidenfeld & Nicolson, London, and Halsted Press, New York, 1973 and 1974; 'Socialism and Ownership' in

Kolakowski and Hampshire (eds.), *The Socialist Idea—A Reappraisal*, Weidenfeld & Nicolson, London, 1974; 'Effects of Adjustment on Competition in International Trade', *Economia Internazionale*, 1976; 'Socialisme du marché et conflits en Yougoslavie', *Revue d'Etudes Comparative Est-Ouest*, Paris, 1977; 'Monetary Union Revisited', *Scottish Journal of Political Economy*, 1977. The IEA published his 'State Control and Competition in Yugoslavia', in *Communist Economy under Change*, 1963, and *Economic Devolution in Eastern Europe*, 1969. He is preparing a book on *Yugoslav Economy under Self-Management*.

PART I

Property Rights, Industrial Democracy and the Bullock Report*

BRIAN CHIPLIN and JOHN COYNE
Department of Industrial Economics,
University of Nottingham

*We would like to acknowledge the comments by Dennis Lees, Arthur Seldon and Ralph Harris on an earlier draft of this *Paper*.

B.C. and J.C.

I. THE ECONOMICS OF INDUSTRIAL DEMOCRACY

'Industrial democracy' is the term applied to a wide range of ideas of which the common element is the extension of the decision-making process within an enterprise away from a single body and towards the whole work force. It represents a recognition of 'rights' of workers, as providers of labour, to participate in decisions, and take part of the responsibility they necessarily imply, alongside the nominated management derived from the body of shareholders as owners of the capital.

It is by no means a new term, nor a new idea: it was an important facet of early theories of socialism, John Stuart Mill regarded it as an inevitable development in the evolution of the enterprise, and it was the title of a classic study by Sidney and Beatrice Webb. More recently it has provided titles for works by Professor Hugh Clegg and Professor Paul Blumberg, and has been used by the Institute for Workers' Control to describe their aims.[1] No one would pretend that its use in all these sources was based upon a common definition. Which ideas does the term embrace?

Bullock's narrow definition

In its most recent use in the title of the Bullock Committee Report[2] it has been applied in perhaps as narrow a sense as possible. It has been chosen to describe a means of placing employee representatives on the boards of major UK private companies, and of UK-established subsidiaries of foreign-based companies.[3] This is simply one form of industrial democracy. In its totality we may consider it as describing a continuum of participative degrees stretching from an unregulated capitalist form at one extreme to perhaps a model approximat-

---

[1] J. S. Mill, *Principles of Political Economy* (1871), Book IV, Chapter VII, University of Toronto Press edition, 1965.

S. and B. Webb, *Industrial Democracy*, Longman, Green, 1897.

H. Clegg, *A New Approach to Industrial Democracy*, Blackwell, 1960.

P. Blumberg, *Industrial Democracy, The Sociology of Participation*, Constable, 1968.

Institute for Workers' Control, for example:

K. Coates, 'Co-determination in Britain', *Bulletin of the Institute of Workers' Control*, No. 10, Nottingham, 1973.

K. Coates and T. Topham, *Industrial Democracy in Great Britain*, MacGibbon & Kee, 1968.

[2] *Report of the Committee of Inquiry on Industrial Democracy*, Cmnd. 6706, HMSO, January 1977.

[3] By 'major' is meant companies with more than 2,000 employees, to which the legislation would apply if the Bullock proposals were implemented.

[15]

ing to the Yugoslav system of worker self-management at the other.[1] These two poles may be regarded as embodying opposite formulations of property rights. In the capitalist form they rest with external shareholders as owners of capital. In the communist form they rest with the workers who collectively own the assets of the plant. Between these two poles lies a whole range of possible democratic extensions of worker participation applicable at several levels within firms, amongst which we would find a group of alternative models applicable to the Board of Directors. The debate on the introduction, or extension, of industrial democracy is essentially about the choice of a position somewhere between the two extremes.

Four propositions

The arguments for the introduction of revised enterprise decision-making along participative lines are based upon several propositions.

The first, which attracts supporters because of its intrinsic appeal, is based upon concepts of social justice. It is 'right' that all concerned in production should have a say in its management: why should ownership of capital lead to an exclusive right to direct both capital and labour? The argument is well expressed in the opening statement to the International Labour Organisation (ILO) symposium on 'Workers' Participation in decisions within undertakings'[2] delivered by the Norwegian Minister of Labour, Mr Leif Aune. He declared that

> 'workers' participation is based on fundamental concepts of justice . . . the ordinary worker invests his labour and ties his fate to his place of work. For this reason he has a legitimate claim to have a share in influencing various aspects of economic policy'.[3]

Some would go further and point to the relative immobility of labour as against share capital as a reason for arguing that labour should have a principal say in the firm's management.

[1] Dr L. Sirc describes the Yugoslav experience in Part II of this *Paper*.

[2] Proceedings of this symposium are reported in the ILO's Labour Management Relations Series No. 48, *Workers' Participation in decisions within undertakings*; the symposium was held at Oslo on 20-30 August, 1974.

[3] Quoted by Johannes Schregle, *International Labour Review*, January-February 1976.

Whatever the validity of the 'social justice' school, it has a good deal of support.[1]

A second argument is proposed on the grounds of improved industrial relations within the firm as a result of decisions being made at least in part by the workers themselves.[2] This argument seems to accept a unitary view of relations in the enterprise as opposed to the more commonly held 'pluralistic' view which acknowledges that the basic objectives of management and workers are essentially at variance.[3]

A third argument, allied to the second, is that worker motivation will increase through their involvement in the enterprise, and that as a result of reduced 'alienation' productivity advances will be made, thus improving the economic performance of the enterprise. The relationship between motivation and economic efficiency is difficult to disentangle, but it is certainly not as straightforward as this simple assertion would suggest. There is a strong body of argument, strands of which formed part of the CBI's evidence to the Bullock Committee,[4] that the time involved in operating participative management decisions could reduce economic efficiency.

These arguments perhaps wane in comparison with the fourth proposition, that the extension of industrial democracy is fundamentally a political question and is being proposed purely because it is electorally expedient to do so.[5]

Industrial democracy in Europe

The debate thus can be seen to encompass reasoning on social, industrial relations, economic and political grounds. A further

[1] The EEC green paper, 'Proposal for a Fifth Directive to co-ordinate the laws of member states as regards the structure of sociétés anonymes', states its position on this matter in positive terms: '. . . those who will be substantially affected by decisions made by social and political institutions *must* be involved in the making of these decisions' (our italics).

[2] 'Difficult problems of industrial relations will be easier to solve properly, fairly and with a minimum of wasteful confrontation, if there are mechanisms which involve those closely affected in the process of finding solutions'. (EEC 8/75, p. 9.)

[3] Alan Fox, *Industrial Sociology and Industrial Relations*, Research Paper 3, Royal Commission on Trade Unions and Employers' Associations, HMSO, 1966.

[4] *CBI Evidence to the Bullock Committee*, March 1976.

[5] Whilst the government is dependent for the success of its economic policy on the acquiescence of the trade union movement, it does not seem illogical that they should seek to implement processes which the TUC in its *Interim Report on Industrial Democracy* (1973) argued were necessary. To quote, the TUC said 'New forms of control are needed'.

significant factor in the desire to embrace participative structures comes from looking abroad, particularly at the experiences of our partners in the European Economic Community. It is currently popular in many spheres of economic life to point to the advances as an industrial trading nation made by West Germany since the early 1950s and to propose emulation. Worker participation is no exception. It is undoubtedly true that the stable operation of participative structures in German industry since 1951 has led to an increase in the popular appeal of such schemes in Britain, although it is by no means proven that co-determination has been even a significant factor in this performance. In justification for the stand it later takes, the Bullock Report itself quotes the 'experiments' in industrial democracy in Germany and Sweden, and the fact that since 1972 the EEC has been grappling with proposals to change European Company Law to impose common models of participation.

The report states categorically that

'It is worth emphasising that the UK is not stepping out of line with other European countries in introducing board level representation.' (p. 54, para. 41)

It is argued here that the Report misread many facets of this European experience.

European comparisons are not easy because of the differences in company law and in company structures. A British public company headed by a single board of directors, for instance, is quite different from its French counterpart, the *société anonyme*, headed by an administrative council (*conseil d'administration*) and a supervisory council (*conseil de surveillance*). Nevertheless, we can make some general observations regarding the nature of the management structure (two-tier board or unitary), the size of firms to which participation relates, and the extent of the employee representation.

First, only five of the nine EEC members have employee representation on the boards of directors of public companies. In one of them, the Netherlands, the involvement is rather indirect: the employees simply participate in the appointment of independent members to the supervisory council (*raad van commissarissen*) in a two-tier system. Of the other four, Denmark and Luxembourg have a one-tier board system, Germany and France a two-tier board system. In Germany the first moves were in firms in the coal and steel industry. The Co-determination Act of 1951 provided that employees and shareholders should elect equal numbers to the supervisory board with an independent chairman (5+5+1). This arrangement was extended by the Co-determination Act of 1956 to include firms with more than 50 per cent of their turnover from coal and steel. All companies in the rest of industry with more than 500 employees were covered by the Works Constitution Act of 1952, which provided that the Supervisory Board comprise ⅓ employee and ⅔ shareholder resprentatives. In 1976 a Works Constitution Act extended these proportions towards equality in firms with more than 2,000 employees where shareholders and employees now have equal representation except that the chairman has a decisive casting vote. In the other countries, the situation varies from France, where two representatives are elected by workers to sit only in a consultative capacity on the Administrative Council, through Denmark, where two representatives have full rights, to Luxembourg where up to ⅓ of the administrative council can be employee representatives. Even in West Germany, it is important to point out that the possibility of deadlock is alleviated by the existence of either a single independent board member, as in coal and steel, or a chairman after the 1976 legislation, whose casting vote would be decisive in deadlocks.[1]

The size of companies to which the legislative proposals apply also varies. In Denmark and France the provisions apply to all companies with more than 50 employees; in Luxembourg the lower limit is 1,000 employees. The Netherlands is again slightly out of line in specifying not only the number of employees (more than 100) but also the amount of capital (at least 10 million guilders). In Germany, as noted, three limits apply: all companies in coal and steel, companies with more than 500 employees in the rest of the economy since 1952, and more than 2,000 employees since 1976.

No common European criteria

On the three criteria of board type, company size, and depth of board penetration there is thus no common European

[1] The ability of the board to make decisions, the authority to do so, and the autonomy of the chief executive have been issues in the European debate. The French Sudreau Commission, which we may regard as the French equivalent of Bullock, remarked that whilst recommending an extension of the board representation for employees to ⅓ it should not go beyond this proportion or else it would severely hamper the ability of that board to make decisions.

[19]

standard. The details are tabulated in Table I. The choice of board is of central importance in the UK debate. The relative merits of the two basic forms (one-tier and two-tier), and a third alternative are discussed in a paper by the Industrial Participation Association.[1] The essence of the debate is whether conflicts of interest can be adequately reconciled within a one-tier board, and whether they would affect the efficiency of management, or whether they could be avoided by a separate management board for day-to-day running, leaving them to be resolved in a higher Supervisory Board. The sides taken in this debate are often based upon ideological differences about the efficacy of unhindered capitalism. However, we must be concerned with it in this *Paper* because the representative strength on a unitary board is an important facet in analysing the attenuation of property rights.

In questions of industrial democracy, the relevant choice concerns the selection of a point on the continuum of participative degrees and, if it is board level representation, the type of company structure to be adopted. The terms of reference of the Bullock Committee can now be examined as they influence the range of options considered.

The Bullock terms of reference

The terms of reference of the Bullock Committee, announced by the Secretary of State for Trade, Mr Peter Shore, in the House of Commons on 5 August, 1975, were:

'Accepting the need for a radical extension of industrial democracy in the control of companies by means of representation on boards of directors, and accepting the essential role of trade union organisations in this process, to consider how such an extension can best be achieved, taking into account in particular the proposals of the Trades Union Congress report on industrial democracy as well as experience in Britain, the EEC and other countries. Having regard to the interests of the national economy, employees, investors and consumers, to analyse the implications of such representation for the efficient management of companies and for company law.'

This remit had caused understandable controversy before it was known that the minority report was to make a criticism of it in the first point in their dissension. The remit contains a

[1] *Works Councils, Employee Directors, Supervisory Boards—A Guide to the Debate*, IPA, 1973.

TABLE I

ESSENTIAL FEATURES OF BOARD LEVEL REPRESENTATIVE STRUCTURES IN MEMBER-STATES OF THE EEC COMPARED WITH THE UK BULLOCK COMMITTEE PROPOSALS

	Type of Company Board Structure	Company Size Applicable (employees/capital)	Extent of Employee Representation	Principal Legislation by Year	Special Features/Remarks
DENMARK	One-tier	50	2 members on board in addition to shareholder nominees	Danish Companies Acts 370-371, 1973	Plans to extend participation through a 'Wage Earners Investment & Profit Fund'
GERMANY	Two-tier	C+S all 500 others now 2,000	5 reps. equiv. to no. of shareholders reps. (5+5+1)	Co-determination Act 1951; Co-determination Act 1956; Works Constitution Act 1952; New Act 1976	Current parity the result of a long process of change
FRANCE	Two-tier	50	2 members on administrative council in consultative capacity only	Works Constitution Ordinance 45-280, 1945	Sudreau Commission recommended an extension to max. of ⅓ rep. Remarked on need to preserve autonomy
LUXEMBOURG	One-tier	100 or where 25% govt. stake in company	⅓ board members or 1 per 100 employees, with min. of 3 to max. of ⅓	Company Law 1974	General govt. opposition to parity
NETHERLANDS	Two-tier	1,000/10 million Guilders	Help to appoint independents	Company Law 1971	Union dissatisfaction leading to demands for extension
ITALY	Two-tier*	—	—	—	No plans to introduce participation unless EEC forces it
IRELAND	One-tier				
BELGIUM	Variant on Two-tier				
UK Bullock proposals (?)	One-tier	2,000	Equal number of employee and shareholder reps. with a smaller group of independents	New legislation to be proposed (?)	Industrial Democracy Commission to be set up as Adviser & Conciliator

*Optional 3rd Board

Source: Employee Participation & Company Structure, Bulletin of the Economic Community (BEC) Supplement, 8/75.

[21]

commitment to a line of action that must inhibit the full exploration of the subject. The minority report remarked that many issues were circumvented because the question was asked in terms of *'How . . .* an extension can best be achieved' rather than *'Whether . . .'* Furthermore, a contentious directive was given to the Committee that any extension would be at board level. It appears that the Committee as a whole, not only the signatories of the minority report, may have felt constrained by these terms of reference. In several places we see that the Committee purposely faced this difficulty and, for a time, widened the terms of reference for themselves, particularly on the level of employee representation. Here the Committee considered an extension below board level, feeling that it was a necessary step to take, even if it was outside the remit. Yet the terms of reference must have given the Committee's deliberations a very strong push in one direction.

The terms of reference also singled out the TUC proposals for special consideration. There was a strong implication that if the Committee were to reject these proposals they would have to justify their position very forcefully, whilst other submissions could be dealt with less seriously.

The terms of reference, therefore, can be seen to have been drawn up very tightly to direct the Committee's attention along clearly predetermined channels. This precision undoubtedly made the writing of the final report much easier than it would otherwise have been, and the logical flow of the report owes much to it. We must, however, consider whether the outcome may have been too much dependent upon the remit, and whether by directing attention to stated aspects of industrial democracy it led the committee to omit consideration of others more fundamental.

II. PROPERTY RIGHTS AND INDUSTRIAL DEMOCRACY

In recent years increasing attention has been paid by economists to the way in which the prevailing system of property rights in a community influences economic behaviour through its structure of penalties and rewards. The essence of the approach is to show that the distribution of property rights affects the allocation and use of resources in specific and predictable ways. This approach offers insights into the operation of a complex

[22]

economy and the relationship between law and economic behaviour. It specifically illuminates the implications of the proposals for extending industrial democracy. Yet it was curiously neglected in the Bullock Report. The failure to recognise this fundamental issue has resulted in recommendations which may have effects far different from those anticipated.

The nature of property rights

Ownership (property right) of an asset, *whether by private individuals or the state*, is regarded as consisting of the following rights:

to use it;

to change its form and substance; and

to transfer all rights through sale (or some rights through rental).

The owner of the property right is rarely allowed unfettered use since some restrictions are generally imposed by private contract or law. Thus, property rights are generally attenuated and the extent of this attenuation has important implications for economic behaviour.

One of the pioneers of the systematic analysis of property rights, Professor Harold Demsetz of the University of Chicago, now at the University of California, Los Angeles, has expressed the principle as follows:

'Property rights are an instrument of society and derive their significance from the fact that they help a man form those expectations which he can reasonably hold in his dealings with others. These expectations find expression in the laws, customs and mores of a society. An owner of property rights possesses the consent of fellowmen to allow him to act in particular ways. An owner expects the community to prevent others from interfering with his actions, provided that these actions are not prohibited in the specification of his rights.

'It is important to note that property rights convey the right to benefit or harm oneself or others. Harming a competitor by producing superior products may be permitted, while shooting him may not. A man may be permitted to benefit himself by shooting an intruder but be prohibited from selling below a price floor. It is clear, then, that property rights specify how persons may be benefited and harmed, and, therefore, who must pay whom to modify the actions taken by persons.'[1]

[1] Harold Demsetz, 'Toward a Theory of Property Rights', *American Economic Review, Papers and Proceedings*, May 1967.

In the light of this formulation it is not surprising that much of the analysis has centred on the question of *externalities*, i.e. benefits conferred or costs imposed on other members of society as a result of decisions, agreements, contracts between individuals and/or governments. Much of the discussion among economists of property rights had been concerned with the *costs* of exchanging, policing or enforcing such rights. For our purposes in this *Paper* the most cogent illustration relates to the role of property rights in the evolution of the firm as an organisational structure.

Some 40 years ago Professor R. H. Coase of the University of Chicago[1] analysed the economic reasons for the existence of the firm as a separate organisation. Transaction costs took the centre of the stage in his analysis as it was necessary to explain why the firms replaced the price mechanism by decision-taking through administration by committees, rules, standing orders, and so on. In the Coase analysis it was the costs of using markets together with uncertainty that explained the development of the firm which dispensed with internal pricing. A firm will then tend to expand until the costs of organising an extra (marginal) transaction within the firm become equal to the costs of carrying it out by exchange on the open market or of organising it in another firm. A general case can be presented that the use of markets is preferable over internal supply where the market works well:

> 'An intermediate market will be said to work well if, both presently and prospectively, prices are non-monopolistic and reflect an acceptable risk premium, and if market exchange experiences low transaction costs and permits the realisation of essential economies. To the extent that the stipulated conditions do not hold, internal supply becomes relatively more attractive . . .'[2]

Incentives for efficiency[3]

Although providing a profound insight, the Coase analysis was not concerned with the implications for industrial policy, and it has been left to others to build on his foundation. One notable

---

[1] 'The Nature of the Firm', *Economica*, 1937.

[2] Oliver E. Williamson, 'The Vertical Integration of Production: Market Failure Considerations', *American Economic Review, Papers and Proceedings*, May 1971.

[3] A similar treatment may be found in A. T. Peacock, 'The Political Economy of the "Dispersive Revolution" ', *Scottish Journal of Political Economy*, November 1976.

contribution is that of Professors Armen Alchian and Harold Demsetz.[1] They introduce the concept of team production where the essence of the problem is that it is difficult to assess the contribution to output of any one member.

The output of a team is not solely the sum of the outputs of each individual, but to make best use of the inputs it is necessary to introduce a reward structure somehow related to effort. Clearly, if rewards were unrelated to effort, there would be no incentive (or, if negatively related to effort, they would induce sabotage). Thus, in the Alchian/Demsetz view, the two key demands placed on an economic organisation are to monitor both the productivity of, and the rewards to, inputs. If an individual input owner is concerned with more than income, for instance, if his/her utility is determined by both income and leisure, team production creates the opportunity for a member of the team to substitute leisure for productive work. Membership of a team implies that any individual does not bear the full cost of his actions. Thus the opportunity and incentive is created for 'shirking' behaviour. The output of the firm will consequently be less than it could be. If such shirking is to be controlled, a monitor must exist who has sufficient incentive not to shirk himself. This incentive could be the right to residual rewards. Thus to minimise shirking behaviour Alchian/Demsetz argue that a bundle of property rights must be invested in the monitor:

1. to be a residual claimant;
2. to observe input behaviour;
3. to be the central party common to all contracts with inputs;
4. to alter the membership of the team; and
5. to sell these rights.

This bundle of rights defines the ownership of the traditional free-enterprise firm.

In 1975 Professor Oliver Williamson[2] presented a devastating analysis of the limitations of simple organisations where all workers are considered equal and there is no recognised

---

[1] 'Production, Information Costs, and Economic Organisation', *American Economic Review*, December 1972.

[2] *Markets and Hierarchies: Analysis and Antitrust Implications*, The Free Press, New York, 1975.

authority, and developed a more widely-based case than Alchian/Demsetz for the emergence of the complex hierarchical organisation. One major task is to provide sufficient incentive to encourage maximum output at minimum cost. In the Alchian/Demsetz scheme the residual reward is essential to provide this incentive for efficiency. But, in modern industry, ownership is divorced from control. If individuals act in their own interest, managers and employees will seek to divert wealth from the owners. In large-scale enterprises the controls which owners can impose on management are limited.[1] Diffused ownership, the minimal impact of one shareholder, and the implied rise in policing costs reduce the element of control. The outside discipline on directors which might be imposed by competition has largely been eroded in many markets by the substantial increase in market concentration which successive governments have initiated (in a range of measures from induced mergers in motor-cars to marketing boards in agriculture) or in which they have acquiesced. Even the potential impact of foreign competition has been eroded by tariff or other protection (and latterly by the falling exchange rate). The market for corporate control (the take-over mechanism) provides perhaps the only substantial discipline on managerial discretion, and even here there are considerable doubts about its efficiency.[2] The liquidation of at least the larger enterprises remains the exceptional occurrence whose rarity is enhanced by industrial 'lame duck' policies.

The tendency in recent years has been for the continual attenuation of the property rights of resource owners, particularly those entitled to the residual reward who might be deemed those with the strongest incentives to secure the efficient operation of British industry.

It is more than coincidence that the attenuation of property rights has coincided with the development of the 'British Disease'[3] which has weakened industry, worsened industrial relations, and reduced the ability to adapt to change and meet the requirements of a modern industrial society.

[1] For instance, Brian Hindley, 'Separation of Ownership and Control in the Modern Corporation', *Journal of Law and Economics*, April 1970.

[2] For example, Ajit Singh, 'Take-overs, "Natural Selection" and the Theory of the Firm', *Economic Journal*, September 1975.

[3] A diagnosis and cure are suggested in G. C. Allen, *The British Disease*, Hobart Paper 67, IEA, 1976.

Growing importance of institutional investors

One fundamental development much neglected in the ownership and control literature is the growing importance of
institutional investors.[1] In the UK this has been most marked
in recent years. Thus in 1963 individuals, executors and
trustees resident in the UK owned 59 per cent of the quoted
ordinary shares in UK companies but British financial institutions (insurance companies, pension funds, banks, unit trusts,
etc) had enlarged their holding to 28 per cent. By 1973 the
institutions had further increased their share to 42 per cent
and the holdings of individuals, etc had fallen to the same
figure.[2] If the attenuation of owners' property rights is a
fundamental cause of 'the British Disease' the role of financial
institutions is of prime importance. It certainly seems true that
they have not been an adequate substitute for private investors,
perhaps because they themselves are primarily managerially
controlled enterprises and traditionally have been rather
reluctant to interfere with the management of companies in
which they own sizeable slices of the share capital. Even if they
wished to exercise more control they face substantial difficulties
in doing so.[3]

There are the political anxieties emphasised by Professor
Richard Titmuss some 20 years ago[4] concerning the potential
abuse of power arising from the concentration of personal
savings into the hands of a small number of institutional
investors. Furthermore, large individual institutions would find
it difficult to dispose of their holdings in companies in which
they are losing confidence without driving down the share
price and facing the possibility of substantial capital losses.
The arguments for and against more active intervention by
the institutional investors suggest no simple solution but it is
to be hoped that they will be at the centre of the deliberations

[1] Although this *was* given attention in early IEA writings, for instance in Arthur
Seldon, *Pensions in a Free Society*, 1957, and *Pensions for Prosperity*, 1960.

[2] The remaining shares are held by charities, non-financial companies, the public
sector and foreign residents. Royal Commission on the Distribution of Income
and Wealth, Report No. 2, *Income From Companies and Its Distribution*, Cmnd.
6171, HMSO, 1975.

[3] Kenneth Midgley, *Companies and Their Shareholders—the Uneasy Relationship*,
Institute of Chartered Secretaries and Administration, 1975.

[4] 'The Irresponsible Society', in *Essays on the Welfare State*, 2nd edn., Allen and
Unwin, 1958.

[27]

of Sir Harold Wilson and his Committee on the working of the financial system.

A whole panoply of government controls and regulations has been introduced in recent years. Incomes policies, the Social Contract, price controls and dividend restraint are merely the tip of the iceberg. The output of regulations, both British and EEC in origin, has continued at a rapid pace.[1] The freedom of individuals to exercise choice has been severely restricted in all walks of life: in consumption, occupation, investment, etc. Much of the intervention has succeeded in weakening the incentive to effort and it is not surprising that efficiency has suffered. The ability to work less intensively for the same reward and to enjoy a 'quiet life' provides short-run benefits to those employed in such circumstances, but as a result consumers, and the national well-being in general, have suffered.

The increased attenuation of property rights which has tended to accelerate 'the British Disease' has also led to a decline in the number of employees who can be sustained at current wage-rates.

Restrict or extend property rights?

That property rights in the modern corporation are attenuated is therefore no argument for their further weakening. Indeed the reverse; some restoration of the rights of ownership is essential if 'the British Disease' is not to reach its terminal phase.

This is not a matter of ideology. Rewards and penalties are the prime movers in human endeavour. Reductions in the incentives to effort produce short-run gains to those fortunate enough to be employed in such circumstances, but at a heavy price in re-distribution of income from consumers to some producers and the long-run costs through continued decline in national ability to produce.

Employee capitalists and market socialism

It has been argued above that the payment of residual rewards is vital to ensure the efficient operation of an enterprise.

---

[1] According to a report in the *Guardian* (21 April, 1977), the Lord's Prayer contains 56 words, the Ten Commandments 297 words, and the American Declaration of Independence has a crisp 300 words; the EEC directive on the export of duck eggs contains 26,911 words.

There is no theoretical necessity for this residual to rest with traditional shareholders or capitalists. There is no objection, in principle, to the employees of the enterprise becoming the 'capitalists', which is the essence of the worker-managed co-operative in market socialism, or market syndicalism. Indeed, it was cogently argued by Mr Peter Jay in his Wincott Lecture[1] that granting ownership and ultimately control of enterprises to the people who work in them may be the only way to prevent a slide into anarchy or totalitarianism.

Market syndicalism is characterised by a pattern of property rights whereby the ownership of productive assets is vested in the labour which applies itself to those assets. In other words, the factory machinery and tools in production in an enterprise are owned by the labour force.

This system contrasts with both capitalism, where capital is often owned by a third party in no way intimately involved with its application other than to collect their portion of the due residual and to risk the loss of the principal, and state socialism, where all assets are owned by 'the state' which acts as the custodian of the property rights for all members of an economy whether they work with those assets or not. Market socialism as an economic system has been the subject of much attention, both theoretical and practical. The practical aspects have been discussed in a substantial body of literature based on the Yugoslav experience where workers' self-management has been in operation for over 25 years.[2] The theoretical work has grown out of, and built upon, early work of economists such as A. P. Lerner, Oskar Lange, E. F. M. Durbin and H. D. Dickinson who formalised socialist ideas to produce an economic analysis of a socialist system.[3] More recent work by B. Ward, E. Domar, J. Vanek and J. Drèze has specifically analysed the operation of worker-owned and -controlled firms

[1] *Employment, Inflation and Politics,* Occasional Paper 46, IEA, 1976.

[2] Discussed by Dr Sirc in Part II. A useful review and reference list may be found in F. H. Stephens, 'Yugoslav Self Management 1945-74', *Industrial Relations Journal,* Winter 1976/77.

[3] O. Lange, 'On the economic theory of socialism', in B. Lippincott (ed.), *On the Economic Theory of Socialism,* University of Minnesota Press, 1938; H. D. Dickinson, *Economics of Socialism,* Oxford University Press, 1939; A. P. Lerner, 'Economic theory and socialist economy', *Review of Economic Studies,* 1934; E. F. M. Durbin, 'Economic Calculus in a Planned Economy', *Economic Journal,* December 1936.

buying and selling within conventional markets.[1] The four earlier analysts developed the theory in a partial equilibrium framework, whilst Drèze has attempted to apply their work in a Walrasian general equilibrium setting.[2]

The important issues in economic terms for market socialism are the efficiency of the system, the way the firm reacts to market signals as compared or contrasted with the capitalist entrepreneurial firm, and the role that the apportionment of property rights has in both these processes.

The essential residual in capitalist and worker-owned firms

We may specify the objective of the firm in both instances as the maximisation of a residual from production. In a capitalist firm it is the profit after all costs, including payments to labour in wages, have been met. In the worker-managed enterprise it is the sum left over to be divided amongst labour after the interest, hire, and depreciation charges have been made against the capital.

Worker management in theory . . .

This difference has implications for the equilibrium employment of labour (membership of the worker-managed enterprise). Whereas in a capitalist firm employees continue to be hired so long as their marginal contribution to the firm's revenue exceeds the wage paid to them, in the co-operative firm the workers are allowed to enter the co-operative only whilst their contribution continues to raise the surplus per head of all the members. Thus they are allowed in until their marginal contribution equals the average earnings per worker.[3] This difference, Professor J. E. Meade points out, matters only in the short term, as in the long run both systems tend to the same equilibrium providing there is free and costless entry and exit for firms.

[1] B. Ward, 'The Firm in Illyria: market syndicalism', *American Economic Review*, Vol. 48, No. 4, 1958, pp. 566-589;
E. Domar, 'The Soviet Collective Farm as a Producer Cooperative', *AER*, Vol. 5, No. 4, 1966, pp. 734-57;
J. Vanek, *The General Theory of Labour Managed Market Economies*, Cornell University Press, 1975;
J. Drèze, (for example) 'Some Theory of Labour Management and Participation', *Econometrica*, Vol. 44, No. 6, November 1976.

[2] An excellent synthesis of the partial equilibrium approach, building particularly on the work of Vanek, can be found in J. E. Meade, 'The Theory of Labour Managed Firms and of Profit Sharing', *Economic Journal*, March 1972, pp. 402-28.

[3] (*See facing page.*)

It is in the short run that responses to, for instance, price changes differ in the capitalist and worker-managed firms. In contrast with the capitalist firm, the self-managed firm would be inclined to reduce its membership when the price of the product rises, so that the residual shared out represents even more to each remaining member. If workers so dismissed can form new enterprises and enter the same industry, the long-run implications for employment and output are the same as in the capitalist economy. It is characteristic of the market socialist economy that it is made up of a larger number of firms, whose average size is smaller than capitalist counterparts would be.[1]

These responses, combined with those expected under imperfect market conditions, where worker-managed firms would tend to be even more restrictive, combine to make the macro-economic management of the economy a very complex business.

Because the worker-managed firm responds by creating unemployment and not employment as a short-run response to a price increase, we may expect the fluctuations in the economy from the monetary or fiscal manipulation of money demand to be more severe in the worker-managed than in the entrepreneurial economy. Maintenance of the economy at full employment, as Professor Vanek has pointed out, may be easier, in the absence of a built-in wage-cost inflation

---

[*See page 30*]

[3] X = units of product
P_x = price of product
L = labour input
K = capital input
P_k = price of capital
i = market rate of interest
W = wage-rate (Capitalist)

For capitalist firm: equilibrium employment of labour where

$$P_x \frac{(\partial x)}{\partial L} = W$$

For self-managed firm: equilibrium employment of labour (membership of firm) where

$$P_x \frac{(\partial X)}{\partial L} = \frac{P_x X - i P_k K}{L}$$

equilibrium of capital is the same for both:

$$P_x \frac{(\partial X)}{\partial L} = i P_k K$$

[1] J. E. Meade, *op. cit.*

mechanism, but at levels less than this the process could be complex.[1]

Making similarly unrealistic assumptions about the make-up of the economy (free and costless entry of firms, universal and freely available 'pure knowledge', etc), Professor Drèze of the University of Louvain also demonstrates that in general equilibrium the two contrasting distributions of property rights (entrepreneurial v labour-managed firms) produce the same long-run solutions.[2]

. . . and in practice: the impact of risk

In theoretical terms, then, with the use of certain (restrictive) assumptions, the two systems can be seen to produce the same responses to given market signals. Since we are concerned with reality we must extract those elements which give us an indication of the probable real-world situation, or at least guidelines to what theory cannot tell us.

The theory proves inconclusive on the respective abilities of the two systems to respond to risk and little is said about the sharing of losses in labour-managed firms. Professor Meade appears to suggest that the entrepreneurial system has as its essence the acceptance of risk to an asset in the expectation of a profitable reward for taking the risk. He notes:

> 'While property owners can spread their risks by putting small bits of their property into a large number of concerns a worker cannot put small bits of his effort into a large number of jobs. This presumably is a main reason why we (traditionally) find risk-bearing capital hiring labour rather than risk-bearing labour hiring capital'.[3]

These theoretical considerations do not, however, give a full insight into the day-to-day internal functioning of the firms. Indeed such a change in the allocation of property rights from entrepreneurs who take risks to employees who are more averse to risk-taking, or who cannot take risks, raises serious problems for the running of these organisations. The property rights approach accurately predicts the problem of the Yugoslav experience discussed in detail by Dr Sirc elsewhere in this *Paper*.

[1] J. Vanek, *op. cit.*

[2] 'The prices of commodities and the remuneration of labour play the same role and lead to the same equilibrium solutions under labour management as under profit maximisation.' (J. Drèze, *op. cit.*)

[3] J. E. Meade, *op. cit.*

There is another major difficulty in sharing rewards: the size of the participating group. As the number of members grows, each individual has a stronger incentive to shirk, partly because the contribution to total effort of any one person falls and, also, shirking becomes more difficult and expensive to detect.[1]

Thus profit-sharing is most appropriate for small teams. It is commonly contended by its supporters that worker participation in decisions solves the problem of the alienation of the work force. If this view is conceded, it does not follow that substantial attenuation of the property rights of resource owners is the way to achieve it. Furthermore, the effect is not always beneficial, for, as one expert on the Yugoslav system has put it:

> 'Alienation caused by feelings of lack of control over his work situation is reduced and efficiency is encouraged. However, it is possible that the ordinary worker may become so frustrated with his experience of self-management that his alienation will increase.'[2]

III. THE IMPLICATIONS OF BULLOCK

In our view the property rights issue is central to the question of industrial democracy. A change in the distribution of property rights or any substantial alteration of existing rights is likely to have a profound impact on economic behaviour. Unless the property right implications are thoroughly examined, the end-result of any recommendations may be far from achieving the desired objectives and may even work in a perverse direction.[3]

Argument

The Bullock Committee in its majority report chose to dismiss these complex issues in a single paragraph:

[1] Alchian and Demsetz, 'Production, Information Costs and Economic Organisation', *op. cit.*

[2] L. Haddad, 'Efficiency and Industrial Democracy: The Yugoslav System', *Journal of Industrial Relations*, December 1975.

[3] An excellent demonstration of these problems in relation to Yugoslavian reforms is in Eirik G. Furubotn and Svetozar Pejovich, 'Property Rights, Economic Decentralisation, and the Evolution of the Yugoslav Firm, 1965-72', *Journal of Law and Economics*, October 1973.

'Before we turn to the issues themselves, it may be helpful to narrow the ground by setting out our position on the views we described as strongly ideological at the beginning of the last chapter. On the one hand, given the existence of a sizeable private sector in the United Kingdom economy in which private capital plays and is likely to play an essential role, we did not discuss industrial democracy in terms of enterprises managed solely for the benefit of employees. Nor are we called upon to express any view on arguments that the private sector should be diminished by an extension of public ownership. On the other hand, it seems to us (as it did to most witnesses) that to regard the company as solely the property of the shareholders is to be out of touch with the reality of the present-day company as a complex social and economic entity, subject to a variety of internal and external pressures, in which the powers of control have passed from the legal owners to professional management.' (p. 41, para. 2)

There are several flaws to be noted in this pronouncement. First, it has been argued above that the issues are not ideological. Changes in the structure of property rights have real influences on economic performance. The property rights approach is one aspect of the recent re-emergence of comparative institutional analysis by economists in which they attempt to assess which alternative real-world institutional arrangements seem best able to cope with economic problems. It is the comparison of alternative real-world arrangements rather than the comparison of an imperfect entrepreneurial with an ideal worker-management method (the nirvana approach) which marks the significant contribution of analysis based on property rights. To dismiss the subject as merely one of ideology is a total misunderstanding of the basic position.

Second, the approach fully recognises the attenuation of property rights and the problems raised by the divorce between ownership and control. But we can predict the consequences for economic behaviour and performance. Similarly any change in existing rights will have predictable effects. The demonstration that property rights are attenuated is no argument for their further attenuation.

The fundamental analysis required is thus to assess the implications arising from the change in property rights which must result from an extension of industrial democracy. Once the problems are recognised, steps can be taken to minimise any harmful consequences and emphasise the beneficial elements. The difficulties should be recognised and not swept under the carpet. In assessing the Bullock proposals, therefore, our view is that the failure to recognise the major fundamental issue seriously weakens the whole analysis of the Committee. It is hoped that the public debate before legislation will not make the same mistake and deteriorate into irrelevant acrimony on ideology and ignore the relevant analysis of economics.

It is true that the Committee's terms of reference pushed them a long way in the wrong direction. They were asked to consider *how* to achieve an extension of industrial democracy, not *whether* it should occur. Yet, even within this pre-judged framework, measures may be proposed to minimise the attenuation of property rights.

Recommendations

The Bullock Committee produced a majority report signed by seven of the 10 members; a note of dissent on a key issue signed by one of the seven; and a minority report signed by three (industrialists) on the Committee. The main general recommendations of the majority can be summarised as follows:

1. Employees in companies with 2,000 or more employees would have the right to elect through trade union machinery a number of employee representatives equal to the number of shareholder representatives to sit on the main policy board of the company.

2. A third group would sit on the board consisting of an odd number (but more than one) of co-opted members jointly elected by the worker and shareholder representatives. This is the $2x+y$ formula where x is the number of worker (shareholder) representatives and y is the number of co-opted members where y must be less than x.

3. To implement the worker representation process requires that a union or group of unions recognised on behalf of grades which constitute at least 20 per cent of a company's employees requests a ballot of employees to ascertain whether they wish to exercise their right to board representation.

4. For the ballot to be successful requires not only a simple majority in favour but that such a majority should represent at least one-third of all eligible employees. Thus, for instance, a 50 per cent turnout would require at least a 2:1 majority (i.e. $33\frac{1}{3}$ per cent of the electors voting 'yes' and $16\frac{2}{3}$ voting 'no').

[35]

5. If the ballot is successful the unions are left to arrive at an agreed procedure for the election of representatives. Thus the representative machinery must be conducted through union channels alone.

6. Joint union committees (Joint Representation Committees) to organise elections to the board and to link board representatives with the normal union machinery.

7. Since it would be both impractical and undesirable to introduce a two-tier board system, employees should have the right to be represented on the present one-tier boards of UK companies.

8. An Industrial Democracy Commission to provide information and advice, formulate codes of practice and generally assist in the implementation of the proposals.

The note of dissent reflects a fundamental disagreement over the composition of the board and the treatment of groups of companies.

The authors of the minority report opposed the terms of reference of the Committee, but given these terms of reference their main recommendation was for a supervisory board of which one-third would be employee representatives, one-third shareholder representatives and one-third independent members. These proposals, as in the majority report, would apply only to companies with more than 2,000 employees, and candidates for the board would be elected by secret ballot, the only qualification being 10 years service with the company.

Implications

'One of the disturbing features of the majority Bullock Report is the impression it gives that its proposals are in the mainstream of European thinking, and that they have a kind of "wave of the future" inevitability about them, especially in the context of our membership of the European Community . . . We have to come to terms with co-determination in some form or other, but we should not adopt an otherwise unsatisfactory model, because we misread the European experience'.[1]

This is the verdict of Mr Michael Shanks, the former Director-General for Social Affairs of the European Commission. In our view this 'misreading' takes the form of a failure to recognise the essence of the arrangements introduced in other countries

[1] Michael Shanks, 'Workers on the board: are we misreading the European experience?', *The Times*, 15 February, 1977.

[36]

in Europe. The essential which the Bullock Report did not understand, and which was also overlooked by Mr Shanks, is that most of these arrangements, whilst providing employees with a useful voice and an ability to influence decisions, *minimise* any attenuation of property rights as a result of employee representatives.

The majority describe, without recognising its significance, how the West German system of two-tier boards was developed in the last century in specific response to demands that *shareholders* should supervise more closely the work of management. This development took place long before the introduction of employee representation. Supervisory boards in German industry were specifically designed to *strengthen* the exercise of property rights, not to *weaken* them, as the majority recommend.

An important aspect of the majority report's views on the role of shareholders is expressed as follows:

> 'One of the weaknesses, it seems to us, in continental countries which have adapted their company law to permit employee representation is that they have introduced employee representation on boards without also considering how the powers of shareholders are affected: and the result of this has sometimes been a reduction in the effectiveness of employees' involvement at board level.' (p. 80, para. 26)

The fallacy in this argument is that it totally ignores the potential contribution to the efficient running of enterprises provided by the residual reward. If the powers possessed by the recipients of residual rewards to monitor behaviour are significantly reduced, the likely result is a further reduction in the efficiency of enterprises. To prevent this consequence it is essential that the incentives provided by existing residual rewards should be replaced from some other source. It can be argued that if employees and shareholders are to be granted parity in decision-taking they should also be given parity in residual rewards.[1] In other words, workers should share directly in any gains (*and losses*) stemming from their actions. Whether such a change in the assignment of rights would be more or less effective than the vesting of majority power in the shareholders is an open question.

[1] The Swedish Meidner plan proposed by the Swedish trade unions in 1976 to support employee representation envisaged that the unions should share in the fortunes of the industrial enterprises through a special fund. Ultimately the unions would gain a controlling interest.

The majority of the Committee were clearly unaware of the crucial part played by sharing gains and losses in encouraging the efficient operation of the enterprise. *The potential conflict between the objectives of employees (including managers) and those of the shareholders cannot be avoided.* Indeed it is one of the main engines of progress. The development of managerial theories of the firm[1] is based on the premise of this fundamental conflict. It is this which keeps management on its toes and contributes to the effective monitoring of the organisation. The majority neglected this fundamental aspect:

'It has also been objected that no change in the law is necessary, since shareholders and employees have the same interest in the continuing effectiveness and profitability of the enterprise, and one set of interests therefore includes the other. Generally speaking, we see the directors' duty to act in the best interests of the company as one of balancing a number of interests, and we agree that there is a large measure of coincidence between the interests of shareholders and employees.' (p. 84, para. 39)

It might be objected that the approach which is being outlined reflects what Professor George Stigler has called a 'tunnel vision of output'.[2] This criticism is unjustified: contracts of employment (including those of managers) are generally specified in loose terms and allow considerable discretion, subject to several controls, notably competition in product markets and, perhaps more significantly, competition for jobs. The potential competition from new entrants to jobs, rivalry for promotion and the desire of employees to preserve mobility provide incentives for good performance. But how will this performance be judged? Employees will, in general, be seeking to impress those other employees (managers) making the key decisions on hiring, promotion and other factors affecting their welfare. As noted above, the objectives of managers and shareholders frequently conflict and competition for jobs, far from forcing performance towards cost minimisation and profit maximisation, may, in practice, encourage the reverse.

For many reasons the controls operated by shareholders are likely to be only loosely binding on managers, and the exercise of discretion is to be expected. This discretion imposes costs on

[1] A recent review is in Michael Crew, *The Theory of the Firm*, Longmans, 1975.

[2] G. J. Stigler, 'The Xistence of x-efficiency', *American Economic Review*, March 1976.

others (e.g. in the form of reduced profits, higher prices, etc) and, if these penalties are avoidable, which they are in many cases, they are rightly counted as costs. The property rights approach emphasises efficiency in the allocation of resources and this is essential if 'the British disease' is to be cured.

Since the Bullock majority failed to recognise the important issues, it not surprisingly proposed the $2x+y$ formula. But its consequences could be disastrous. In a penetrating criticism of this aspect of the report Mr Peter Jay wrote:

'Management by compromise between basically conflicting objectives—at its worst management by deadlock—is not a coherent basis for running anything, unless perhaps it be a committee (and the world market for the kind of "camels" they produce is distinctly thin).'[1]

Although it seems persistently to be neglected, the essential purpose of an economic system remains the optimum allocation of resources to the satisfaction of consumer preferences. A viable alternative to traditional entrepreneurial capitalism that should be given serious consideration is to transfer property rights to the workers in an enterprise. It presents substantial difficulties, as examination of Yugoslavian experience shows (Sirc, Part II). In the British economy employee entrepreneurship must remain a long-run possibility. The danger of a Bullock-type compromise is that it will accelerate the downward spiral to such an extent that few worthwhile assets would remain for transfer to the workers. The difficulties with the idea of workers' co-operatives as a remedy for some of the problems of the modern corporate state need sensible airing, not outright dismissal. A compromise that removes the last vestiges of any remaining exercise of property rights is no solution to the fundamental problems facing the economy.

The dissenting note by Mr N. S. Wilson, a solicitor, went at least some way towards recognising the dilemma. He noted that the $2x+y$ formula creates many complex problems, particularly in relation to groups of companies. He saw no objection to shareholders retaining a majority on the board and suggested that the number of employee representatives should be determined by a strict formula based on the number of employees in a company without any limitation on the composition of the remainder of the board.

[1] *The Times*, 27 January, 1977.

The property rights issue is the fundamental economic flaw in the Bullock analysis. There was also the strange notion of democracy embodied in the majority recommendations. The workers would express their preferences on two basic questions: first, the decision whether to adopt the principle of worker representation; second, if adopted, the selection of representatives.

The system is triggered at the request of unions and a ballot of employees is held, generally at the company's expense, in the company's time and on company property, thereby giving employees every chance to vote. But the majority recommended that those eligible to vote should be all full-time employees, including short-time or laid-off, but *not* part-time employees. Further, they suggested that in industries with high labour turnover, unions and employers might like to stipulate that employees should have a minimum period of service in the company before being eligible to vote. Ironically they said it was desirable that as few people as possible be disenfranchised but presented no case for excluding *any* employees.

The argument on high labour turnover is to a large extent a red herring. If a firm has high labour turnover it does not follow that any individual new employee is likely to stay for only a short period. Furthermore, there is no corresponding requirement that shareholders should have held their shares for a minimum period before being eligible to vote. In general, women have a somewhat higher turnover than men; they would be unfavourably affected by the committee's recommendations. In addition, most part-time employees are women; it is not clear that they are necessarily less interested in the operations of the company simply because they are part-time. Given that there is no case in the Report for the exclusion of any employees, this suggestion cannot be taken seriously.

Male chauvinism?

The selection of representatives was to be left entirely to the unions; non-union members were totally excluded from the process. The majority report stated that the proportion of non-union members is generally small in the larger companies affected by the proposals and most of these are white-collar employees. These are no reasons for disenfranchisement.

Furthermore, a much higher proportion of women than

men are non-union members and non-manual employees. About 57 per cent of male employees belonged to unions in 1974 compared with 37 per cent of females. Two-thirds of women are employed in non-manual occupations compared with one-seventh of men. Again, the proposals clearly have the effect of disproportionately excluding women.

In an era of general universal suffrage in Britain it seems an astonishing suggestion that numbers of workers should be arbitrarily disenfranchised. It is amazing that in the first year of the Sex Discrimination Act the majority of the Committee should propose legislation that is blatantly discriminatory against women. It is to be hoped that the Equal Opportunities Commission will have something to say on this apparent Bullock or trade union chauvinism.

To include the term 'industrial democracy' in the title of the Report is therefore a gross misrepresentation. This is a flaw recognised in the minority report:

> 'It is one of the great strengths of political democracy in the free world that every citizen has equal political rights and that no one has to belong to a particular party or organisation in order to exercise those rights. No citizens have to demonstrate their belief in collective representation before they can vote for a representative in Parliament. It would make a mockery of democracy as we know it to limit the rights of employees in any system of industrial democracy to those who have opted for collective representation through a Trade Union.' (Minority Report, p. 175, para. 25)

Public choice and the rules governing the representatives

The peculiar view of democracy adopted by the majority has obscured a significant issue which was given no consideration in the Report. This concerns the selection of appropriate decision rules and their effects on the behaviour of the elected representatives. There is an important and growing body of economic literature concerned with the issue of public choice which recognises that the policies pursued by elected representatives are heavily influenced in general by the implications they have for the probability of re-election.[1] The analysis of an indirect democracy through representatives is complex but it

[1] For instance, Gordon Tullock, *The Vote Motive*, Hobart Paperback No. 9, IEA, 1976; for a comprehensive summary of the literature, Dennis C. Mueller, 'Public Choice: A Survey', *Journal of Economic Literature*, June 1976.

is clear that a 'first past the post' system is unlikely to be the most desirable process of selection. The significance of this point in relation to German experience was cogently expressed by Professor Gerald Lawson of the Manchester Business School in a letter to *The Times*:

> 'The spirit of co-operation in Germany springs from several sources, of which worker participation is probably the least significant. These sources include . . . the superior system of electoral democracy in Germany which, with one exception, has produced coalition governments throughout the post-war period, all of which have pursued highly stable centrist political and economic policies.'[1]

It is disturbing that this aspect of the problem was not even considered by the Bullock Committee.

A further consequence of the proposals of the Committee relates to the implications for employer-employee relations, which may be more complex than the Report suggests, discussed in IV.

IV. EMPLOYER-EMPLOYEE RELATIONS

An essential argument of the majority is that employer-employee relations are improved to the benefit of both parties. Employer and employee would remain meaningful terms, even after Bullock, because in the absence of an explicit transfer of property rights their respective status remains unchanged. The resultant increased economic efficiency may bring financial rewards to both parties, and the employee may further benefit from the feeling of involvement in the working environment.

Will employee 'participation' improve industrial relations?

It is false to believe that an improvement will *necessarily* come about by an extension of 'industrial democracy', but it is important to examine the potential beneficial effects for industrial relations. Such an improvement is not a natural consequence of merely redefining the internal organisational arrangements within a firm. Success depends very much upon the manner in which 'participation' is exercised, and the forms it takes. Whilst 'alienation' at work might be considered to be

[1] *The Times*, 14 February, 1977.

a major factor placing a brake on worker productivity, frustration with a participative structure inappropriate to the enterprise or distant from the individual worker may increase alienation rather than remove it.[1] Caution of this kind formed part of the conclusions that Professor Malcolm Warner came to in a recent article:[2]

> 'Simply installing participative structure as such will not be sufficient; nor will the simple transfer of forms from another society *in itself* produce participative behaviour.'

The form of participation is therefore an important determinant of its success. In judging an extension, and particularly the proposals in the Bullock majority Report, we must consider the recommendations in the light of existing employer-employee relations and the pertinent trends in their development.

Changing character of collective bargaining

In the UK the major way in which workers have sought to influence their working environment is through collective bargaining, which may be defined in its widest form to include joint negotiation not only about substantive issues such as the immediate wage-work bargain but also about the authorship of rules regulating other aspects of work such as internal mobility/flexibility, safety, welfare, etc.[3] Some commentators regard this as a form of participation in management.[4] We would argue this is not so. Through collective bargaining, unions simply seek to delimit the sphere of action within which management can make decisions without employees/unions accepting part of the responsibility,[5] which remains firmly at management's door. Participation in the form in which this *Paper* and Bullock consider it necessarily requires *joint* responsibility of directors/managers and rank-and-file employees for a large number of major decisions.

[1] J. Obradovic, 'Participation and Work Attitudes in Yugoslavia', *Industrial Relations*, February 1970.

[2] 'Whither Yugoslav Self Management?', *Industrial Relations Journal*, Spring 1975. Professor Warner is Professor of the Joint Graduate Programme, Brunel University and Administrative Staff College.

[3] This definition is therefore wider than that used by, for instance, Professor W.H. Hutt in his recent Hobart Paperback No. 8, *The Theory of Collective Bargaining 1930-1975*, IEA, 1975.

[4] N. W. Chamberlain, *Collective Bargaining*, McGraw-Hill, New York, 1951.

[5] This has been very successful for trade unionists, and many prefer the clearly defined lines of demarcation that collective bargaining offers them.

This process of collective bargaining has developed considerably both in content and breadth of employees covered. It has also been characterised by an increasing emphasis on local involvement and the strength of shop stewards as 'grass roots' representatives. Workers have increasingly identified themselves with their most immediate means of representation, and there has been a power shift within the trade union movement away from full-time officers towards shop stewards. National issues of inflation, wages, health and safety, unemployment and the 'social contract' have given national leaders more prominence over the past two years, but it is significant that pressure for new pay policies begins by articulation of workers' dissatisfaction through local shop stewards and joint shop stewards committees.[1]

Importance of the 'grass roots'

What this 'shop floor' identification emphasises is the need for participation to build upwards from the bottom, through the involvement of all workers, if it is to be a success. If there is alienation, this is where it is felt, where productivity advances may be made, and where workers have demonstrated their involvement.[2] The importance of middle management, which is vital to the efficient operation of the organisation in controlling production, and the relationships formed between them and employees, is ignored by the Bullock Committee. This may cause difficulties through replacement of fears of 'alienated' workers by the reality of alienated management who will feel disfranchised if the representative structure bypasses them.

The Bullock proposals reflect a misreading of this trend. Implementing procedures distant from the workers is contrary not only to what evolutionary trends might have suggested were important in the UK but also to the European experience, which developed statutory participative structures at lower levels in advance of, or at the same time as, representation on boards of directors.[3] The forms of lower-level participation in

[1] The Leyland shop stewards were the first to press actively for a return to free collective bargaining in 1977.

[2] The majority Report, in discussing evidence submitted to it on these and related matters, points out that there already exist in *some* companies participative structures which have been a natural voluntary evolution.

[3] Arndt Sorge, 'The Evolution of Industrial Democracy in the Countries of the European Community', *BJIR*, November 1976.

Europe are shown in Table II (p. 46). The Committee may be absolved of total responsibility for this omission in so far as its terms of reference directed them towards board representation. They did consider lower-level participation, agreeing that

'What is needed is an inter-related structure of participation or joint regulation at all levels of the enterprise, and a sufficiently well-developed structure of participation below the board is clearly vital.' (p. 41, para. 3)

But their conclusion that the statutory implementation of board representation would strengthen existing lower-level structures and provide an impetus for the development of participation in companies where there is currently a vacuum may be questioned.

Employer-employee preference for voluntary agreement

The development of collective bargaining in the UK has been marked by the general preference of both employers and employees for non-legalistic agreements and as little government intervention as possible. Just as the Industrial Relations Act of 1971 was the target of trade union opposition because of legislative intrusion into previously unfettered areas, so the Bullock proposals could become an equivalent target for employers, although their bargaining power is weaker. This absence of statutory intervention contrasts sharply with the situation in Germany where legal regulation of industrial relations has been accepted over a long period. If there is to be an acceptance of statutory involvement without a radical transfer of property rights, it must be gradual for employer-employee relations to improve. A strengthening of evolutionary trends favouring local involvement, possibly as a first step towards a fully integrated structure, would therefore be preferable to a major legislative leap in at the top. The arguments the Committee considered, but did not endorse, about the 'training ground' for would-be representatives to get experience cannot be so lightly ignored.

Conflict between union representatives

The industrial relations scene is often disrupted by conflict, not between the traditional adversaries, management and unions, but between unions. The TUC has an important role

[45]

TABLE II
FORMS OF WORKER PARTICIPATION BELOW BOARD LEVEL IN EEC COMPANIES

	Extent	Applicability	Method of Choice of Reps.	Powers
BELGIUM[1]	Enterprise Councils — 50% mgmt. 50% employees	Firms of more than 150 employees	Secret Ballot; TU may nominate candidates	Discuss: (1) alterations to work conditions (2) Recruitment (3) welfare (4) lay-offs (5) work rules
DENMARK[3]	Co-operative Committees — 50% mgmt. 50% employees	Firms of more than 150 employees	Elected shop stewards are *ipso facto* employee reps.	'Co-influence' on (1) day to day prdn. and work planning (2) alterations (3) local work and welfare (4) staff policy
GERMANY[1]	Works Council — All employee reps.	Firms of more than 5 employees	Secret Ballot of all employees	Social, staff, & economic matters. Conduct of employees, working hours. Rights of participation & co-determination in a wide range of matters
FRANCE[1]	Enterprise Committees — 3 to 11 employee reps. plus chief executive	Firms of more than 50 employees	Secret Ballot on proportional representation basis	Entirely consultative except for social welfare policy. Must be consulted on redundancies, employee work changes, etc.
IRELAND[1]	Safety Committees — Various forms	Workers in all factories have the right to set them up	Various	Limited to discussions of safety under Factory Act 1955
ITALY[2]	Works Councils — All employee representatives	All firms	Secret Ballot of all members but TU's do nominate candidates	Represent employee interests at all stages. No formal *power*
LUXEMBOURG[1]	Mixed Committees — 50% employees 50% mgmt.	Firms of more than 150 employees	Elected by personnel delegates by Secret Ballot	Participation in admin. of welfare programme
NETHERLANDS[1]	Enterprise Councils — Up to 25 members depending on size of firm	Firms of more than 100 employees	Ballot of employees TU's can nominate candidates	Must be consulted on matters pertinent to employees, e.g. pensions, working time, holidays, safety and health

Sources: *Employee Participation and Company Structure*, BEC Supplement 8/75; International Labour Organisation, *Workers' Participation in Decisions within Undertakings*, ILO, 1976.

[1] Set up by legislation. [2] Set up by agreement with unions and employers but confirmed by Act in May 1970.
[3] Set up under an agreement between Danish Federation of Trade Unions and Danish Employers' Confederation.

of conciliation between independent member unions.[1] This situation has often been referred to as a 'problem' of multi-unionism and was one subject of the Donovan Report.[2] Multi-unionism can take two forms: first, where two or more unions in a plant represent different classes of worker, and second, where they recruit the same class of worker. The former is more common, and implementing the Bullock proposals, giving the JRC the task of deciding how the employee representatives should be elected on to the board, might prove more problematic than the Committee realised.

Non-employee trade union representatives

An important aspect of the debate is the qualifications of employee representatives.[3] The Committee said that whilst employee representatives would normally be members of the company, it would not want to exclude the possibility of full-time trade union officials unconnected with the firm from joining the board as direct employee representatives. In the nature of democracy, and the attenuation of property rights, this seems a most unusual aspect of the proposals, in keeping with many features of the Report by a Committee whose terms of reference precluded them from analysing the pros and cons of industrial democracy.

V. CONCLUDING REMARKS

'If the right solutions can be found, the benefits to the nation, to industry and to individuals will be enormous; a misjudgement could lead to disaster'. (Minority Report, p. 170, para. 2)

We have charged Bullock with a serious misjudgement stemming from a failure to recognise the importance of the role of property rights. An acknowledged major problem in the modern corporation is the attenuation of property rights arising from the divorce between ownership and control. Industrial democracy as interpreted by Bullock would further

[1] TUC annual reports generally begin with statistics on the number of disputes referred, and the action the TUC has taken in principal disputes. Many more arise and are settled before reaching this stage.

[2] *Royal Commission on Trade Unions and Employers' Associations Report*, Cmnd. 3623, HMSO, 1968.

[3] Bullock Report, Chapter 10, paras. 38-39.

weaken these rights with potentially damaging consequences. The role of residual rewards or 'profits' in ensuring efficient production is vital, whether they are received by 'capitalists' or 'workers', and the failure to recognise this analysis of incentives is at the heart of our criticism of the Bullock Report.

The terms of reference totally failed to take account of these critical issues or permit them to be aired. For its part, the Committee did not consider how the attenuation of property rights could be restricted to the minimum consistent with the terms of reference. The Committee seemed wholly to misread the European experience.

We agree with the Committee:

'. . . that the problem of Britain as an industrialised nation is not a lack of native capacity in its working population so much as a failure to draw out their energies and skill to anything like their full potential.' (p. 160, para. 2)

But, in our view, the essence of this failure stems from the attenuation of property rights, which would be worsened rather than improved if the Bullock recommendations were carried out.

Bullock's missed opportunity is an issue of much wider significance than 'industrial democracy'. In recent years the consequences of much government policy have been significantly to reduce incentives to effort and innovation. This trend must be reversed if there is to be any hope of curing 'the British disease'.

PART II

Workers' Management under Public and Private Ownership*

LJUBO SIRC
University of Glasgow

*I wish to thank Professors Armen Alchian, Gordon Tullock and Tom Wilson, Mr Geoffrey Denton and Miss Sarah Ludford, Mr Robin Milne, Mr Ken Smith and Dr David Watson for commenting on the first version of this paper. Mr Arthur Seldon, Mr John Wood and Mr Michael Solly have obliged me by their editorial and production work. The views and mistakes remain my sole responsibility.

L.S.

I. ABOVE AND BEYOND BULLOCK

The majority report waves aside the problems of workers' management, which can be predicted theoretically and which have emerged in Yugoslavia, the only economy where full management by workers has been tried for 25 years.

Decisions without responsibility

The majority (and the minority) report disregards the complications of entitling sectional interests (as opposed to parliament and judiciary) to participate in decisions about property they do not own, and to overrule the owner-shareholders with the help of the third (Y) group on the board. At worst this arrangement means that the property can be transferred from owners of an enterprise to the sectional interest of its members, at best that some of the decision-makers are in no way economically responsible for their decisions. If an enterprise makes losses, the value of its capital falls, while the workers whose representatives have participated in the decision, or have even caused it, continue to expect payment of market wage-rates.

Directors' responsibilities unenforceable

Economic responsibility is not discussed at all. When it is said that the board with workers' participation should 'carry the ultimate responsibility for decisions in important areas of strategic policy', 'responsibility' means 'jurisdiction' for which no sanction (responsibility) is foreseen. The directors are recommended to have the fiduciary duties of loyalty and good faith and the duties of care and skill: but, according to the report itself, these legal duties are difficult to enforce in court, as it is also difficult to prove fraud by directors. In practice, the real economic responsibility would continue to fall ultimately on shareholders who would lose their capital, while they would not have the right at law to dismiss those causing their loss.

Conflict of employees' and the public interest as consumers

The majority report says that 'the power of individual shareholders to sell their shares remains' (p. 80). This naturally misses the point. If the owners and/or their representatives are no longer able to ensure that their capital is put to the best use (but only to get rid of it at a lower price), the whole basis of a decentralised economy is undermined.

[51]

This development would not only be to the detriment of shareholders, over whose loss no tears are shed in our day when the functions of ownership are misunderstood. It would also damage the general public (workers as consumers) in whose interest capital should not be frittered away but invested where it produces most output. This general interest conflicts with the sectional interests of the employees in continuing in the same job although it no longer pays because, for example, there is insufficient demand for its products, or to have continued investment in their enterprise although investment elsewhere may contribute more to welfare and output.

This goes also for capital invested abroad. It may be desirable from the general point of view, from the point of view of workers as consumers, that capital be invested abroad, not in the plant which has accumulated it, because returns on foreign investment may pay for imports of inputs, particularly raw materials, which are necessary for the functioning of an economy, possibly for the very working of the plant whose workers resent investment abroad. Especially an economy like the British, without much natural resources, must be—and was —geared to earning a part of imports by returns on capital and entrepreneurship deployed abroad. It is very shortsighted to claim that profits must be invested where earned.

The interests of employees

The majority report recommends that all directors should be required to act in the interests of the company's employees as well as its shareholders but does not explain what it means. Directors have always been obliged in law to take account of the interests of employees in the sense that they had to implement the contract of employment which specifies the employees' claims on the company in exchange for performing the duties of their jobs. Furthermore, directors always have to consider the legal and moral framework within which the company operates. This implies that the workers are, *grosso modo*, paid the going time- or piece-rate and that it will rise because of competition for their services between employers, when the general efficiency of the economy or their part of it increases.

Any right in excess of that means that workers are paid different rates in different enterprises—which they will resent, that accumulation is eroded, and possibly that capital is used inefficiently from the point of view of workers as consumers. This third result seems to be what the majority report has primarily in mind, because it recognises as a possible source of divergence that employees may argue for priority to be given to employment. It does not say over what interest employment should have precedence, but in practice it is bound to be over the efficient use of capital by keeping enterprises working at a loss and using capital for covering losses. Such a priority may not matter much if tolerated temporarily or exceptionally, but it must harm a country's economy if it becomes widespread. In the final result, it would stop progress. Employment should ideally be preserved, but it can be preserved efficiently only if workers move to new jobs when the old ones are no longer economically required. This is in their own interest: preservation of uneconomic jobs eventually destroys the basis for the rise in wages that most workers ultimately want.

The majority report misunderstands the working of the economy and wants to replace decisions taken within the framework of the 'invisible hand' mechanism with *ad hoc* decisions by special interest groups for their immediate convenience, which in the end must lead to financial chaos, diminished efficiency, and lower living standards than necessary for all. Yugoslavia has amply demonstrated this inevitable consequence.

Short-term and long-term interests of workers

The majority report evaded the question of the low propensity of employees to save, especially if savings do not become their property. Most surveys indicate that the foremost preoccupation of workers is better pay. The natural consequence of average or low income is that their inclination to save is low even if savings become their property. If their savings become state property or the property of others, their propensity to save becomes even lower. They push the company towards a high wages policy (Bullock Report, p. 53). Yugoslavia confirms this diagnosis.

Workers do not do this because they are 'short-sighted' or irrational but because it is in their individual interest as perceived by themselves. They may realise that investment raises their productivity, but they believe there is no need for themselves to put money aside, since they think it will come from somewhere else. That is why the talk about an investment

[53]

strike and about British money being invested abroad persists despite the catastrophic fall in real profits from which investment normally comes. If everything else fails, government is expected to step in and provide investment as if out of thin air. Workers do not seem to realise that they could be regarded as 'free riders' who profit from investment provided by others and prevent them from gaining a return on it.

This attitude prevails in Yugoslavia, where it has resulted over the years in low rates of growth and low rates of capital accumulation.[1] Investment in Yugoslavia is financed out of inflationary issue of paper money. These tendencies have developed because the workers have been given the right to determine accumulation by deciding their 'personal incomes'. In Britain workers do not have that right yet, but the tendencies are in the same direction, as indicated by the recent events in Chrysler, Leyland, British collieries and elsewhere. These are the tendencies everywhere in Western Europe.

The result would not be any different if the workers clearly understood the inter-connection between their wages and investment. It would still be in their personal interest (short-term and long-term) to extract from the enterprise as much as they could and let others pay for investment. This is particularly true because workers are not tied to enterprises for life.

To ignore or blur these conflicts of interests and attitudes, and to talk about 'the worker' as an abstraction without self-interest, reflects muddleheadedness that harms the community, primarily workers themselves. To encourage the workers in insupportable claims sets them against one another because not much more can be extracted from people with high incomes. The 'class struggle' leads to chaos and inefficiency. Marx, in one of his more lucid passages, admitted that

'owing to an increase of productiveness both the labourer and the capitalist may simultaneously be able to appropriate a greater quantity of necessaries [consumer goods].'[2]

This could be called Marx's own case against class struggle, particularly as 'the capitalists' will primarily spend on producer goods, not 'necessaries', which will again contribute, if properly handled, to a further increase in productivity.

[1] Interview with Dr Dusan Anakioski, Yugoslav deputy federal secretary of the market and prices, *Ekonomska Politika*, Belgrade, 14 February, 1977.

[2] R. Freedman (ed.), *Marx on Economics*, Pelican, 1976, p. 61.

Would the unions restrain the workers?

Perhaps the Bullock majority tacitly hoped that any tendency towards insufficient investment and excessive consumption would be checked by the power they proposed to give trade unions over the 'industrial democracy'. Possibly they expected that the trade unions would constrain the workers' singleminded pursuit of higher wages.

Experience suggests they would not. If they did, they would alienate their own members, whom they have been telling for years that a higher standard of living can be provided by pressure on employers or the government. The declarations by leading trade unionists that the government should talk less about wage restraint and more about price control, reduction of unemployment and reflation, indicate yet again that they either do not understand the economics of industry or are not prepared to declare the truth that unemployment overwhelmingly depends on wages. This reluctance of the unions to tell the rank-and-file the truth augurs badly for any kind of TUC policing of capital investment in schemes of industrial democracy.

How would the TUC police capital accumulation and investment?

Even if the TUC could protect accumulation, what would they do with it? Its members on the boards of individual enterprises could not decide because wider views are required for investment decisions. So a general TUC plan would be required which would be no better than other plans that have so far done little but push countries into crises. Efficient investment requires thousands and thousands of individuals with expert knowledge looking for the best opportunities stretching far into the future.

If trade unions are not able to police accumulation, the policing would have to be done by government decree, which would take spontaneity out of the economy and would be a further step towards centralist state planning. The chances are that the government would not only have to decide the amount of accumulation, but would also have to do the investing. And this would lead to the usual inefficiencies in centrally planned economies.

The only alternative is to allow private owners to accumulate and invest. They are then responsible for efficient investment because the value of their capital depends on such efficiency and the penalty for inefficiency may be to reduce it to zero.

[55]

The owners bear such responsibility also if they manage capital through appointees who are to a large extent independent, so that they must have at least the power to dismiss them if the system is to work.

Historic weight of inevitability

The majority report said that a new role for employees within companies is required because of economic trends and post-war higher standards of education and living (p. 22). A prominent member of the majority, Mr Clive Jenkins, went further[1] and claimed that

> 'the thesis that those who invest their lives, blood, flesh, sinews and nervous energy should have a formal place in decision taking must be one which has an historic weight of inevitability'.

The argument on inevitability would have more power of persuasion if it were not that, not so long ago, historic inevitability was claimed for state ownership of the means of production and centralist planning, both of which have failed to produce the results claimed for them.

It is by no means certain that 'the worker' really wants participation in decision-making. Workers cannot all *individually* take part in decisions, while British surveys show that only seven out of 100 on the shopfloor give high priority to workers' directors.[2] Yugoslav surveys confirm this attitude (p. 74). In Switzerland, the idea of co-determination was rejected by the electorate in a referendum in March 1976.[3] Only 39·3 per cent of the enfranchised bothered to vote and of these only 32·8 per cent, that is, only about 13 per cent of the total electorate, voted in favour of co-determination. They rejected both the trade-union proposal and the counter-proposal of the Swiss government.

Educational standards and management

The claim that higher educational standards lead to requests for participation may be questioned. I hope I may consider myself well educated, but nonetheless I feel no inclination to interfere with everything in my institution, although I hope

[1] 'The majority view', *Financial Times*, 8 February, 1977.
[2] *The Times*, 26 January, 1977.
[3] *Neue Zürcher Zeitung*, 23 March, 1976.

that people will treat each other with reasonable respect regardless of their relative position and rank. It is probably my education that makes me realise that some division of labour is required if for no other reason than that time is scarce and that in some kinds of work expertise and experience are required. My education may have influenced my conclusion that democracy is the best solution in political life, but not necessarily applicable to industry (p. 79). My education may also inhibit me from being suspicious of anybody in a position of limited authority until there is evidence to the contrary. I do not view administration as supreme and the seat of power, but mainly as a supporting activity which can be a burden on individuals with other things on their minds. And if anybody in authority tries to harm people who are not, they have the rule of law to protect them.

Such rights and procedures are also available to all workers. In the final analysis, the law has to protect them from one another because even eroding the capital of an enterprise harms not only its owners but also the rest of the community, who are no less investing 'their lives, blood, flesh, sinews and nervous energy' in the economy.

Renewed hopes for a 'new civilisation'

It seems that it is not the workers but trade-union officials who badly want 'industrial democracy'. If they are wrongly accused of wanting it to provide 'jobs for the boys', it is more probable that they wish to take over because they have the limitless but unfounded and unsubstantiated confidence that in their hands everything will be different. Mr Jack Jones expects a 'new civilisation'[1] which is a quaint echo of the high hopes of Sidney and Beatrice Webb when they wrote their book on *Soviet Communism: A New Civilisation*.[2]

I well remember Yugoslav communists when they were similarly confident that immediately after imposing their rule everything would change, but then proceeded to blunder from one system to another and from one policy to the next. President Tito was asked in 1962 whether he felt that the exercise of power was more difficult than he expected and admitted: 'Of course, it is more difficult than I thought. And not only I

[1] *The Times*, 3 December, 1975.
[2] Longmans, 1935.

[57]

thought it would be easier. I believe it is easier to wage war than to organise government and direct social development.'[1]

Living standards and change of system

High living standards could unequivocally be a reason for a change in the system if the majority argued that the standard of living were so high that 'participation' became more important than further rises. There is no evidence that the workers would see it that way; nor is there any evidence that 'industrial democracy' can provide for a faster rise in wages. On the contrary, the higher post-war standard of living would indicate that it is safer to keep the system that has brought it about—private ownership and management of capital independent of employment. Marx highly praised the success of the bourgeoisie that, by his time, had created more massive and more colossal productive forces than all preceding generations together.[2]

Workers' councils: a possible solution

Yet it is true that the relations between workers, management and shareholders have become bad and some remedy has to be found. At least partly the relations are so bad because propaganda has buried the real relationships under heaps of emotive slogans, and some companies are now so large that a man on the shopfloor no longer comprehends their operation.

Workers' councils[3] at all levels, elected by *all* employees, could serve to improve communications. Management could be asked to supply them with information, answer their queries and receive their suggestions and complaints. That is not much, but it is as much as can work. Giving the employees the right of decision-making on an enterprise's capital leads to chaos.

---

[1] President Tito's interview with Henry Fairlie on 18 September, 1962, published in *Queen*, London, No. 5497.

[2] R. Freedman (ed.), *op. cit.*, p. 16.

[3] The term 'workers' council' is used here in a different sense than in Yugoslavia, where it means the basic management board of an enterprise consisting entirely of workers' representatives.

II. THEORY AND PRACTICE OF WORKERS' MANAGEMENT

1. INTRODUCTION

The theoretical study of labour-managed firms was pioneered by Benjamin Ward in his paper 'The Firm in Illyria: Market Syndicalism'.[1] The main elaboration of his approach was *The General Theory of Labour-Managed Market Economies* by Jaroslav Vanek.[2] Both authors mainly concerned themselves with the consequences arising if income (wages+profit) per worker is maximised rather than profit. Their approach has only limited significance because, under conditions of uncertainty about the future, a firm struggles to earn any profits at all, not to tailor them to particular wishes.

It is sobering to check theoretical considerations against actual developments. In Yugoslavia, workers' self-management has been in operation for 25 years. There are considerable differences between Yugoslavia and West European economies, not least between their labour forces, but within Yugoslavia itself conditions also vary so much that its North-Western regions can easily be compared with neighbouring Austria and Italy. An application of Yugoslav lessons to the rest of Europe is thus more plausible and a review of Yugoslav results gives some guidance for other countries.

Dr Vanek and many others use Yugoslavia for their advocacy of workers' management, but his views of Yugoslav developments[3] are so idealistic that he sometimes arrives at theoretical results not warranted by Yugoslav practice. Thus he claims, for example, that

'contrary to the Keynesian system describing the capitalist economy, no rigidity is to be expected here [in labour-managed economies] which would prevent prices from adjusting'.[4]

One of the main features of the Yugoslav system is that workers are not prepared to accept incomes dependent on market results (p. 65).

The Yugoslav market system with workers' self-management certainly functions incomparably better than the central

[1] *American Economic Review*, 1958, p. 566.
[2] Cornell University Press, 1970.
[3] *The Participatory Economy*, Cornell University Press, 1971, Ch. 4.
[4] J. Vanek, *The General Theory . . ., op. cit.*, p. 175.

[59]

planning it replaced in the early 1950s. Nonetheless, basic faults soon appeared. They are discussed under three headings:

(i) blurred responsibility (2);
(ii) inflationary distribution (3);
(iii) power of organisers (4).

Section 5 discusses the concept of industrial 'democracy', ownership by workers, and altruism.

2. BLURRED RESPONSIBILITY

(a) Initiative, continuity and value of capital

Workers' management implies a market economy in which decisions about what to produce and how to produce it are taken within enterprises. Prices and costs indicate the state of supply and demand, and their difference (profits or losses) serves as a sanction: those who have taken decisions to produce cheaply what the public wants are rewarded by profits, those who have not are punished by losses. For the system to work, there must be a clear-cut link between the takers of decisions and the economic consequences. It is not sufficient that *everybody* will be worse off if the decisions are wrong.

With workers' management this link cannot be established because:

1. An enterprise larger than an artisan's workshop cannot be started by an assembly of workers before the plant has been built. The economic initiative must rest elsewhere, either with private entrepreneurs or with political authorities. Workers who join a well-conceived enterprise are simply luckier than those who do not.

2. Consequences of decisions do not follow instantly in established enterprises either. If workers continually join and leave, sanctions will fall on a changing workforce. Employees can avoid the consequences of bad decisions they have helped to take by giving notice.

3. If workers do not own the capital of the enterprise they manage, or do not pay a full market interest rate for its use, they derive an advantage from working with large amounts of capital and will tend to amass it.

Under capitalism without workers' co-determination, equity owners themselves take decisions or delegate them to their appointees, but the risk falls on them in both cases. They are

[60]

rewarded with higher profits or punished with losses. If they wish to give up their stake in an enterprise, they have to sell their share; this process apportions responsibility because the value of the stake varies with the assessment of the enterprise by all interested in acquiring capital. Every time capital changes hands, the value is adjusted for previous mistakes and successes and for future prospects; this market evaluation influences the wealth of those who have been responsible for the decisions.

With workers' management it is impossible to engineer this kind of apportioned responsibility. Workers do not own the capital of enterprises and, if the capital is owned by the state, there cannot be a capital market at all. In Yugoslavia, the introduction of a capital market was discussed in the early 1970s; the idea was dropped for reasons of political principle.

A partial possibility of assuring that workers are rewarded for good decisions they or their representatives have taken and punished for bad decisions would be to prohibit their dismissal and limit their freedom to change jobs.[1] The abolition of the ability to leave would interfere with the free choice of place of work and the abolition of dismissals would make for a completely rigid economy. Another limited solution would be labour markets where workers *buy* themselves into good jobs carrying profit bonuses, and dismissals are linked with compensation.

(b) Privileged and unprivileged workers

Because of this inability to establish responsibility for decisions, it was soon realised in Yugoslavia that self-management was unjust to some workers and gave undue advantage to others. One solution discussed was called 'equalisation of business conditions', but if *all* business differences are abolished the market can no longer work. If it does not matter whether or not an enterprise produces what people want at the lowest possible price, there is no incentive to take the right decisions.

One easily noticeable difference between enterprises—the cause of privileges which tend to produce inequalities among workers—is the amount of capital per worker in branches and factories. For a long time there were attempts to eliminate this difference by government fixing of the interest-like taxes paid

[1] J. E. Meade, 'The Theory of Labour-Managed Firms and of Profit Sharing', *Economic Journal*, 1972, p. 420 ff.

by the enterprises on all their capital. But it was difficult to establish what the capital was really worth without a capital market, so that all sorts of makeshift devices had to be used. Further, rates of interest-like tax had to be low to enable badly planned enterprises to pay them, since there were large differences in capital productivity due to haphazard investment. As a consequence, workers in better enterprises still derived much income simply from their superior equipment.

Finally, interest-tax payments meant that accumulation was taken out of the hands of enterprises and handed over to a political authority, investment fund, or bank, which perpetuated the division between initial and current decisions. But this device was contrary to the principle that all decisions on investment must be taken by the workers themselves. The interest-like tax was, therefore, abandoned in the early 1970s.

(c) Investment allocation

Not only were enterprises with more capital privileged; there were also all the bad consequences of re-investment ('ploughing back'). Ploughing back is often bad practice because investment does not go where it would produce higher returns and contribute most to economic development. By expanding production which is cheapest in relation to its market value, investment leads either to a reduction in market prices or to a rise in wages: both increase the real earnings of the workers in the economy as a whole.

If the workers do not own capital and make decisions about its use, ploughing back surpluses may be the only way open to them. If they are not given a yield on capital invested outside their enterprise, they will not invest elsewhere. It is in their interest to invest in their own enterprise, even if that raises their own productivity only slightly, rather than invest outside where productivity might be increased substantially.

The Yugoslav communist leaders were forced in 1967 to allow payment of interest from one enterprise to another, even though such 'unearned income' was initially thought repulsive. Ideologically, it could be described as 'group capitalism', since groups instead of individuals derived the benefit and became virtually the owners. But movement of capital from enterprise to enterprise was necessary and, human nature being what it is, a payment was required to achieve this movement without a return to the inefficient central direction

[62]

of investment, usually more under the influence of political than of economic criteria.

(d) Possible application to British and other economies with private ownership

If, as proposed by the Bullock report, the workers or their representatives are given a say in the decisions taken by companies, there will also be discrimination between workers according to whether they happen to be in well-run companies or not. The benefits they are presumed to derive must differ from enterprise to enterprise. And since they will not be tied to the enterprise, the consequences of decisions they will help to take will not necessarily fall on them. The most important decisions taken with the co-operation of workers' representatives will, of course, be on investment.

Decisions on capital by non-owners

In Britain and elsewhere groups of workers already have the power—if not the formal right—to force management to invest and use capital in ways detrimental to the owners and the community. It assumes a very negative form: usually management is prevented from closing down or dismissing excess labour—as in steel, docks, newspapers, railways, etc—thus incurring losses, which means dissipating capital. Capital that should be available to increase general productivity is lost in order to enable some employees to avoid changing their jobs. Yet even they themselves would be better off if they allowed capital to be used to create new posts elsewhere.

The excuse often heard in Britain for not allowing an enterprise to close is that the difficulties are only temporary, or that more investment or better management could save it. All these claims are judgements about the future which cannot be objectively proved in advance. The decision on the probable outcome is therefore best left to those who bear the risk, the owners, and who will lose something if the result expected does not come about.

If the enterprise does not close down, and more capital is invested, but losses continue, good money is thrown after bad by the owners who are responsible for losses (which are also resources lost to the community). The owners lose a further part of their capital, i.e. part of their earning capacity which they have acquired in addition to their labour by carefully managing property. This loss should be a punishment for their own wrong decisions, not for those forced on them. Workers in a factory that closes also lose their jobs, but their earning capacity is not reduced, provided they can find another job, which they would if the labour market is allowed to work. If not, their 'right to work' entitles them to unemployment benefits until a job is available. In no circumstances can owners keep a losing enterprise open indefinitely—they would lose all their capital. And state subsidies to keep a plant open are no better than the dole. On the other hand, the workers could take the risk of keeping the enterprise open by paying for the losses out of their wages. But would they accept this arrangement?

A genuine worker-managed enterprise would be one run by workers using their own capital or borrowed capital, paying the interest on it. They would then avoid piling up capital in order to raise their own productivity (at the expense of other people's). The burden of responsibility for their decisions would be squarely on them: any losses would have to be paid by them out of their existing capital or by not drawing wages; and they would have to keep the borrowed capital intact. Would this result be acceptable to public opinion? It would entail workers losing their invested savings or a part of their wages for repaying debts. If not, there would again be no clear-cut responsibility for decisions on investment.

3. INFLATIONARY DISTRIBUTION

(a) *Allocation of revenue in Yugoslavia*

In the 1950s, the right of workers' councils in Yugoslavia to distribute the revenue of enterprises (that is, the value added, usually called 'income') was narrowly limited by all sorts of taxes. Later there were two attempts, in 1961 and 1965, to give workers the freedom to determine how revenue would be divided between individual incomes and investment. Both attempts ended in failure for two reasons:

1. Workers in enterprises (or parts of enterprises) doing badly saw no justification for being paid less than those in highly profitable enterprises.

2. Workers in general had no incentive to leave enterprises with sufficient funds for investment.

(b) *Comparability of workers' incomes*

There is a clash between the requirements of the market in

[64]

satisfying consumer preferences and the way in which workers judge the adequacy of their incomes. The market requires that people who organise production to meet consumer demand be rewarded by higher incomes than those who do not organise enterprises or who let their enterprises incur losses. Workers have usually been shielded in the past from the success or failure of their enterprises in the sense that their wages did not depend in the short or medium term on the performance of the enterprise. They even enjoyed priority when it came to cover debts to suppliers and other creditors, while shareholders were at the end of the queue.

Remuneration and the market

Workers' self-management is different. In Yugoslavia, workers are supposed to run the enterprises themselves. The running of a market economy in these circumstances requires that their wages should be raised if there are profits and reduced if there are losses. But the workers *do not 'perceive' the connection between their remuneration and the market.* At best they are prepared to accept variations in their wages in accordance with changes in *physical* productivity (per unit of labour), but not *economic* productivity depending on how well the goods sell to satisfied customers in the market and the price achieved. This reaction of the workers is understandable, since it can hardly be claimed that, even under self-management, an individual worker can influence the fate of the enterprise.

Yugoslav workers gladly accept high wages if their enterprises happen to work at a profit, but refuse to submit to a reduction if the enterprise suffers losses. On the contrary, they usually insist on parity with workers in profitable enterprises (as do some unions in Britain) or comparability of wages for the 'same kind of work', which is in direct contradiction to their supposed role as risk-taking entrepreneurs. Under the influence of parity, the whole wages structure moves inexorably higher and higher, as 'personal incomes' (wages) in the best enterprises move up and the others follow suit. Some Yugoslav economists consider this hankering for comparability of wages, superimposed on self-management and the market, as the most potent engine of inflation.

The consequences of this development are grotesque. In the 1960s strikes proliferated although the leaders were telling the workers that, under socialism, there should be no strikes

[65]

because when the means of production are in social owner-ship workers can only strike against themselves. To be more precise, they do not strike against *themselves* but against *one another* (which they also do under capitalism). There were strikes against 'low' wages relatively to wages in other enter-prises, strikes against delayed payment of wages when enter-prises were in difficulties, and so on. There were also clashes between—and strikes against—parts of enterprises. A worker (or a minority of workers) in no way feels he (it) makes decisions if they are taken by a majority *against* his (its) vote. He (it) feels exploited by the majority. And Yugoslav communist leaders, particularly Edvard Kardelj (the leading ideologist) in 1972, have admitted that exploitation of worker by worker is possible.

The result is that loss-making enterprises increase their losses and many potentially viable enterprises incur losses. Any project evaluation, economic calculation, and cost accounting become difficult. Wages are not based on produc-tivity in the least successful enterprises, but on labour produc-tivity plus profits of the most successful firms which cannot be foreseen in advance. Even if they could, hardly any enterprise except the most successful could afford to pay them without incurring a loss. The whole system is kept going only by inflation which blurs all economic calculations: annual rates of increase in the Yugoslavian cost-of-living index in recent years were 1970—11 per cent, 1971—16, 1972—17, 1973—20, 1974—21, and 1975—24.[1]

Buoyancy by inflation

The majority of Yugoslav enterprises represent a drainage system through which inflationary additions to the money supply, borrowed to pay for losses, pour out into the hands of citizens. They pay out more in costs, especially wages, than they can ever hope to recover by selling their products. If the inflationary issue is restrained, what the Yugoslavs call 'illiquidity' emerges: many enterprises do not have enough cash to honour their liabilities. This illiquidity then spreads the shortage of money to the whole productive apparatus. The final result is called 'mutual indebtedness'—enormous claims by firms on one another (involuntary credits), which can be

[1] Source: *Yugoslav Statistical Yearbook 1976*, p. 297.

partly cancelled when the government organises 'compensation rounds', but not in so far as they represent bad debts.

The complication is that many enterprises are in difficulty not only because of excessive wages but also because they were misconceived from the start and there is little demand for their goods. The government finds it politically difficult to admit large-scale misinvestment (some economists and observers consider about one-tenth of enterprises to be misconceived), especially as closures would add to unemployment. This mixture of losses partly because of excessive wages and partly because of wrong investment decisions makes re-introduction of financial discipline very difficult.

It has been said repeatedly in Yugoslavia that enterprises would be prevented from obtaining additional money and thus forced to cut their wages and possibly to close down. But the authorities have shied away from this consequence when workers showed their dissatisfaction. In some instances, Communist Party branches themselves ordered banks (presumably illegally) to extend new credits which everybody knew would not be repaid. Moreover, there are other arrangements to keep loss-making enterprises going. They are either given subsidies (out of public funds or joint reserve funds to which all enterprises contribute), or are merged with profitable enterprises.

(c) Insufficient accumulation of savings

Excessive wages as a result of self-management imply inadequate savings. Firstly, the low propensity to save[1] of workers with low incomes means that, if workers themselves decide how much should remain in the enterprise for further investment, the chances are that they will leave much less than would private capital-owners.

Secondly, what capital-owners leave in the enterprise remains their property and adds to the value of their capital. In contrast, whatever the workers under Yugoslav self-management do not take out of 'their' enterprise does not accrue to them personally but to some undefined 'society'. Only so long as it is ploughed back into the enterprise, and they consider their jobs secure or do not wish to leave, can there be some kind of bond, albeit tenuous, between them and the saved funds.

[1] Propensity to save is the inclination to put money aside for future use out of a given income, individual or collective.

[67]

The reactions of Yugoslav workers to the 1965 rule allowing them freely to distribute the enterprise's revenue should not have been entirely unpredictable. Insofar as they can influence the distribution of 'income' they distribute as much as they can among themselves, sometimes leaving the enterprise without capital and 'liquidity'.

Another turn of events was more unexpected. In spite of their low incomes, the workers did not spend all their money on consumer goods but saved it partly to build private houses and partly in saving accounts with banks. In 1974 the rise in private deposits with banks in excess of the rise in private borrowing outstripped collective savings (ploughing back), which on balance tend to be nil, although one cannot be sure how high private savings would be if they were not more than matched by transfer payments by Yugoslavs working in Western Europe to their families in Yugoslavia.

Nevertheless, the Communist leaders were taken aback. They did not expect the private ownership instinct in Yugoslav workers to be so strong. When the tendency to save privately rather than collectively first appeared in the late 1960s, the political leaders moved to prevent it getting out of hand by a kind of 'incomes policy' to cope with 'privatisation' and inflationary pressures.

Ideology and exhortation

Communist ideologists kept repeating that workers would eventually understand that, to increase productivity and production, it was necessary to save and accumulate and would act accordingly. They overlooked not only the possibility of an excessively low propensity to save but, even more important, the complication arising out of 'social' as opposed to 'private' ownership of the means of production.

Workers are aware that savings which pay for investment help to raise their productivity. But, similarly, everybody is aware that at least some government services add to everybody's standard of living in the wider sense of the word. Nonetheless, there are usually no queues to pay taxes that maintain these services—the so-called 'social wage'. Taxation has a close parallel to savings which become 'social property', so that these savings acquire a tax-like quality.

Obviously, investment is required to improve productivity, but as individuals always feel that taxes are excessive so

[68]

individual workers or groups of workers feel that they contribute too much to investment. It is always nicer if somebody else pays taxes, and if somebody else provides investment too. And somebody else does: in Yugoslavia, on the whole, the banks, mainly out of inflationary credit expansion, and this means that eventually everybody contributes.

(d) 'Incomes policy' à la yougoslave

In the late 1960s, the Yugoslav Communist leaders decided that the uncontrolled distribution of enterprise income must stop. But since they had been claiming for years that one can easily arrive at a workable system by handing decisions over to workers, they could not retreat from their previous view by regulating distribution simply through government decree.

They therefore worked out an elaborate system which formally controls payments of incomes to workers by so-called 'self-management agreements'. They are 'negotiated' between trade unions representing workers, chambers of commerce representing enterprises, and the government. In practice, these bodies negotiate very little but adopt schemes prepared by economists. They can also hardly be expected to negotiate, as the three bodies are fully dominated by the Communist Party and therefore do what the communist leadership says.

These arrangements met with less than full success. Accumulation in Yugoslav 'social' enterprises continues to be crowded out by current disbursements, comprising 'personal incomes'. At times disbursements exceed revenue. In 1975 these enterprises made, on average, no profits at all but a loss amounting to 3·6 per cent of their combined revenue.[1] In the first half of 1976, when a policy of monetary stringency was tried, the average loss increased to 13 per cent.[2] There have been on balance losses in all years since 1970. Admittedly, it is difficult to define 'a loss' under Yugoslav circumstances, but the figures nevertheless show a lack of financial discipline and, in consequence, of service to the customer. The explanation appears to be that the workers, while not very interested in self-management, do use all their self-management rights and scope for spontaneous political pressure when it comes to

[1] Milivoje Nikolic, deputy director general of the Social Accountancy Service, 'Financial results of organisations of associated labour in business 1971-1975', Jugoslovenski pregled, 1976, p. 323.
[2] Ekonomoska politika, 29 November, 1976, p. 25.

[69]

'wages'. And in practice the 'incomes policy' itself is used more to prevent differentials than to protect capital accumulation.

Distribution rules imposed from above and, even more, the financing of practically all fixed investment out of bank credits have cut whatever connection between workers' control and investment there may ever have existed. If workers cannot be allowed to decide freely between revenue distribution and savings, they cannot be expected to take much interest in how savings are to be invested. Furthermore, investment decisions are a full-time job which requires considerable knowledge and continuous absorption of vast amounts of information.

Thus investment decisions are largely back in the hands of the government either through banks or through self-management agreements influenced by the Communist Party. The Yugoslav leaders, however, freely admit that these bodies are incapable of taking appropriate investment decisions except in a very limited number of cases. They are excessively exposed to political and social pressures, they do not themselves run any risk, except possibly political, and they simply do not know the investment opportunities in detail. In Yugoslavia, private workshops, which are grudgingly permitted, can make a lot of money because the social sector is so bad at producing whatever is in demand.

The production structure is incredibly distorted. As soon as production is stepped up, about 10 per cent of the total output goes straight into stocks to be written off because of very poor quality or lack of demand. Utilisation of productive capacity is about 70 per cent, in some cases as low as 40 per cent. The mistakes which caused these distortions go back to the time of central planning, but self-management has done little to improve the situation: it simply reproduced the existing faulty structure.

(e) Possible application to economies with private ownership

These consequences of self-management are relevant to developments in Western Europe, although there so far workers have not had any formal role to play in enterprise decisions. The moves to 'worker participation' in various forms have come about because of trade union activity which disregards the economic limitations and effects and rests rather on the political and psychological power of the trade unions. There is the danger that the formalisation of workers' influence on decisions in enterprises with capital owned by others will strengthen the tendencies displayed in the Yugoslav experience and harm everybody, *primarily workers themselves as consumers*. As in Yugoslavia, there is upward pressure on the whole structure of wages. When the British car industry was prosperous, car workers demanded high wages because of high profits, but then the miners also wanted comparable wages despite that mines were making losses. If workers demand higher wages because of profits *and* parity |despite |losses, government must pay subsidies out of taxation or inflationary expansion of money supply, or companies must disinvest (not replace) their capital or borrow, or there must be unemployment. In all cases everybody else's income is reduced because he has to pay higher taxes, or the productive capacity of the country is reduced.

In Britain, the consequences of excessive wage claims and resistance to plant closures show up in the figures for profits:[1] adjusted for stock appreciation and capital consumption, profits fell from just under 13 per cent of net domestic income in 1965 to less than 5 per cent in 1975. This reduction was helped by inflation, which masks the change in real terms. It would not matter so much if the fall in profits indicated redistribution of consumption from the rich to the poor, but it does not. The taxation system, which bears harder on distributed than on undistributed profits, sees to it that most profits are retained and ploughed back, so that a fall in profits means a fall in accumulation. If in 1973[2] all personal incomes over £5,000 after tax in Britain had been confiscated, only about 1 per cent would have been added to the incomes of the rest. And these incomes might then have fallen because of the destruction of incentives.

The role of property rights

All these changes in the West are taking place because people no longer understand the role of ownership[3] and have allowed property rights to become so weak that they no longer play

---

[1] *Bank of England Quarterly Bulletin*, December 1976, p. 415.

[2] Calculated from Board of Inland Revenue, *Inland Revenue Statistics*, p. 45.

[3] E. G. Furubotn and S. Pejovich, 'Property rights and the behaviour of the firm in a socialist state: the example of Yugoslavia', *Zeitschrift für Nationalökonomie*, 1970, p. 28, and 'Property rights, economic decentralisation and the evolution of the Yugoslav firm 1965-1972', *Journal of Law and Economics*, 1973, p. 275; S. Pejovich, 'Towards an economic theory of the creation and specification of property rights', *Review of Social Economy*, 1972, p. 309.

any regulatory role in the economy. Trade union leaders, claiming to speak on behalf of the workers, have had their way to such an extent that they have made themselves a rival force to Parliament and have obtained for the workers *as producers* all sorts of rights without corresponding duties—but not so much at the expense of 'capitalist bosses' and managers as at the expense of *the workers themselves as consumers*. Directors and managers have not disappeared, because under all economic systems there must be somebody to organise production. And, if capitalist bosses disappear, they are replaced by political bosses who may be less experienced and less prepared for their work, so that they continue fumbling for years before discovering that the old solutions were after all unavoidable and even made good sense.

Property rights prevent capital from being eroded and guide it where it produces the best satisfaction of market wants, which is in the interest of the workers as consumers. Private owners and their representatives are, fundamentally, only mediators between the same people in their capacities as producers and as consumers. As producers people have sectional interests, as consumers general interests. Owners' interests are different from those of workers as consumers only in so far as they consume their incomes from investment and do not re-invest it. Such consumption usually happens on a very small scale and is the price we pay for preserving the owners' interest in efficient investment which makes a decentralised economy possible.

The danger of workers' participation is that it may strengthen the tendencies to the erosion and misallocation of investment, already strong and detrimental to workers as consumers.

4. POWERFUL ORGANISERS

(a) Organisation and ownership

Marx and his followers, concentrating on formal ownership, entirely overlooked the truth that what gives day-to-day, as opposed to ultimate, power in an enterprise is not so much formal ownership as organisational ability. Enterprises in all economic systems—communist or socialist as well as capitalist—consist of a large number of activities which have to be co-ordinated and orientated towards the market. Whoever does the co-ordinating is in a position of power which can possibly be transferred to another organiser but not to the mass of employees without destroying the enterprise.

This proposition may seem to be in conflict with the foregoing argument that private ownership safeguards the link between initial investment decision and current decisions, and that it should also prevent disinvestment and insufficient savings through excessive distribution of revenue for consumption. How could either of these results be achieved if organisers (managers) make the decisions?

The separation of ownership from management indeed poses problems and complicates the simpler picture as it existed when management was still primarily in the owners' hands. But, provided the managers are appointed by owners and can be dismissed by them, they are in ultimate control and responsibility also falls on them through changes in the value of the capital and its possible loss. The owners rightly suffer if they have chosen managers who do not protect their capital and if they do not replace them when their inadequacy is revealed.

Certainly large numbers of shareholders cannot do the organisational work themselves, but shareholders' *direct* democracy has never been prominently claimed as one of the advantages of private ownership. Workers' direct democracy, the possibility that they themselves could take all decisions, is on the contrary frequently promised as a feature of so-called 'industrial democracy' and a remedy for 'alienation'. This happens although they obviously cannot do the continuous organisational work themselves but can, at the most, elect organisers to act on their behalf. This is a far cry from the original idealistic hopes. When electing managers, workers will in all probability not be interested in their ability and willingness to preserve capital and invest it wisely, but in their possible largesse in distributing enterprise profits in current income.

Do workers want a voice in decisions or better pay?

Yugoslav Communist leaders have not taken this realistic assessment of the power of organisers into account at all, and have vested organisational jurisdiction in workers and their councils and committees. Neither the workers nor their representative bodies can exercise the right thus given. They know they cannot, and they are not interested in doing so. They cannot because they have neither managerial skill nor the

[73]

necessary information. This is not so much due to their lack of education as to the need for them to do their own job first. Even if the workers do not always understand why, they sense that the rights they have been given are bogus. Yugoslav sociological investigations[1] have shown that they consider workers' councils and other such bodies 'talking shops' while real influence is concentrated in the hands of managers. Investigations[2] have similarly shown that, in real life, what the workers are interested in is better wages and influence on their immediate work environment, not in general decisions such as marketing or investment.

This picture has its obverse side. Because all formal rights were given to the workers, managers in Yugoslavia have become more powerful than ever, since they have real power which is not formally admitted, and, as a result, not regulated in any way. They have power without responsibility, because responsibility implies that sanctions are attached to actions. There are no sanctions for organisers in Yugoslav self-management, since formal responsibility always rests with workers against whom sanctions are very difficult to enforce. Yugoslav firms are sometimes described as 'formally anarchic' by some Yugoslav sociologists.

There cannot be sanctions against workers because collective responsibility is no responsibility at all. People do not feel any link with collective decisions, especially if they have voted against them. They think they are victimised if they are held responsible for results. While shareholders can lose their risk-capital, workers would have to lose part of their 'wages'. But they do not wish to risk their wages. It follows that all consequences in the end fall on the outside community. The state re-insures all enterprises for their losses, which means that there is no pressure on individual enterprises to mend their ways. Everybody thus tries to 'pass the buck' to everybody else; but 'everybody else' is themselves. Instead of a war of 'all against all', this is a war of each against himself.

[1] Leslie Benson, 'Market Socialism and Class Structure: Manual Workers and Managerial Power in the Yugoslav Enterprise', in Frank Parkin (ed.), *The Social Analysis of Class Structure*, Tavistock, London, 1974, p. 264. Benson gives an account of the views held by Yugoslav sociologists on self-management.

[2] J. Jerovsek, *Industrijska sociologija* ('Industrial sociology'), Maribor, 1972, p. 234, and Veljko Rus, *Odgovornost in moc v delovnih organizacijah* ('Responsibility and power in working organisations'), Kranj, 1972, p. 11.

Real power in informal groups

Under these conditions, real power is taken over by informal groups who run enterprises without being responsible for results. For this reason, it does not matter whether they are good at their jobs or not, as long as they are good public relations men who succeed in pleasing both the workers and the party which influences their appointment. It is far more important for a manager in Yugoslavia to have party backing than to have professional qualifications, not only because this helps him to hold down the job but also because it is in the interest of the enterprise under distorted Yugoslav conditions.

The formal rules are so complicated that no enterprise can survive if it observes them. It is necessary to cut corners, which is possible only if the manager has strong political ties. If the enterprise makes losses, a 'loyal' manager can always pull strings and obtain a loan or even a favourable change in the rules, which are continually being altered anyway.

It is thought in Yugoslavia[1] that self-management is mis-applied because it cannot perform an 'instrumental function', i.e. organise purposive action, although it can fulfil the function of 'social integration' or produce social rules on people's activity. But such social ethics do not help with efficiency, which is essential for service to customers: we simply do not know how to help each other in a more complicated society unless other people say what they want, which is precisely what happens through the market. But then we also require professional organisers to make our actions conform to our wants.

(b) Restriction of organisational power

The only solution would seem to be to legitimise the power of organisers and then restrict it by defining it.[2] The Yugoslav government is not keen on that because, *inter alia*, it officially still sticks to romantic dreams about how in the fullness of time both the state and enterprise organisers will wither away. This refusal to face reality makes it almost impossible to find feasible solutions. It is also difficult to limit organisational power in enterprises because entrepreneurial activity includes

[1] J. Zupanov, *Samoupravljanje i drustvena moc* ('Self-management and social power'), Zagreb, 1969, p. 116 ff., and Jerovsek, *op. cit.*, p. 197.

[2] Veljko Rus, *op. cit.*, p. 109, and J. Zupanov, *Samoupravno preduzece* ('Self-managed Enterprise'), Zagreb, 1971.

risk-taking, and evaluation of risk is subjective, so that it cannot be codified.

Back to private ownership?

The ideal solution as considered by some Yugoslav social scientists[1] comes as a surprise. They believe that the best restraint on organisers would be to give them the ownership of the means of production. They do not hope that this solution could be adopted within the foreseeable future, but they are by now clear that private property does not bestow privileges simply, or even primarily, on the owners, but is connected with the need to administer resources efficiently. Efficient administration requires owners to do what is in the interest of consumers and the general interest: to invest where it is most profitable, which means in the production of what people want to buy, at the lowest possible price. The best solution is evidently private ownership of the means of production, combined with trade unions to look after working conditions, and legal and moral rules to prevent everybody from gaining by violent or otherwise immoral behaviour.

(c) Resentment of organisers

It is still difficult to pursue this solution in Yugoslavia or elsewhere. Prejudice against private ownership is rife. Few realise that the present prosperity of leading nations in the world, and civilisation itself, is based on superior organisation. One of the consequences of this general climate is the resentment not of owners but of organisers as such.

The quality of Yugoslav managers is still, on the whole, well below Western standards, but they are one of the main assets of the country. They are the searchers for new products and market possibilities, detectors of comparative advantage, and technical innovators.[2] Despite their beneficial role in the economy, their public image is unfavourable partly because they are considered to be usurpers arrogating to themselves organisational power—which presumably nobody should have —and partly because the authorities tend to use them as scapegoats for failures in substitution for capitalists and even bureaucracy.

[1] Veljko Rus, *op. cit.*, p. 200 ff.

[2] A. Bajt, 'Managerial incentives in Yugoslavia', paper to VIIIth International Seminar organised by CESES in Ermenonville, 13-15 September, 1972.

Resentment of organisers often includes technical experts who are accused of 'technocratism', that is, preventing 'workers' from taking over all decisions by claiming that some decisions require expertise.[1] Experts are sometimes paid less than people without qualifications, and frequently workers refuse to allow the employment of experts because they do not understand their work and begrudge them their higher salaries.

(d) Possible application to economies with private ownership

In Western Europe and North America, a development which may have diverted enterprises from their purpose is the separation of ownership from management. Some managers have used their inherent power and indulged in empire-building, to command ever larger establishments, instead of trying to produce most cheaply goods in demand.

Workers' participation might strengthen this tendency since they could combine with managers in considering everything from the viewpoint of the sectional interests of a company's employees—but disregarding capital owners' interests, which also means disregarding the interests of consumers at large. In so far as some managements do not try hard enough to resist excessive wage claims, this result has already come about. In Britain and elsewhere, it has reduced the share of net profits in net domestic income (p. 71), and has thus cut down the accumulation of investment.

The most unwelcome tendency in the West is the re-investment of a large part of internal funds in the enterprise without due consideration of profitability. It could be restricted if government, instead of encouraging ploughing back, would encourage distribution of profits and thus de-concentration, and the development of smaller enterprises. But this policy, though it would be to the advantage of the public (workers as consumers), would in all probability be resisted by those advocating participation, because it would deprive workers of their co-determination in investment. It would, however, allow capital to flow where requirements are highest, and it would encourage smaller-size enterprises to emerge, possibly the only way to reduce alienation.

[1] R. D. Lukic, 'Between Democracy and Technocracy', *Politika*, Belgrade, 16 May, 1970; B. Dolnicar, and I. Vidic, 'Technocratism on the Sieve', *Delo*, Ljubljana, 12 February, 1972; and P. Bozic, 'The Sources of Conflict between Workers and Technocrats', *Delo*, Ljubljana, 10 November, 1973.

Trade unions in Britain seem to be aware of the danger that workers (and managers) in individual plants could insist on their sectional interests (p. 55), and, therefore, want a leading role for themselves—just like the Yugoslav League of Communists—so that they would partly substitute themselves for market forces, possibly through 'planning agreements', and partly by a strong influence on the board through managers nominated by themselves. They seem to over-rate 'planning', despite its failure in Eastern Europe, and under-rate the skill and, especially, training and experience needed for management.

Workers on boards

What stance would workers' representatives on company boards take in Britain and other countries with private ownership of capital? There are two possibilities:

1. Representatives would be serious people understanding wider issues. They may on the whole agree with the managers and owners, which may make them unpopular with their workmates as long as they do not understand the working of the economy and its requirements. Many of them may never become reconciled with the realities of life if they continue to be fed fairy tales about an enormous surplus-value hidden somewhere and withheld from the workers by capitalist cunning. Participation will have some beneficial effect merely if it helps to make people face the economic facts of life—it will certainly not bring about abundance, which does not depend on easy-made recipes but on superior organisation, responsibility enforced through ownership, and on persistent and intelligent hard work.

The danger is that workers will fall out with their representatives if the election to leading office makes these latter see reality and nothing is done to explain to the workers the first principles of economics instead of distracting them by slogans about 'exploitation' and 'alienation'. Indeed, workers may become alienated from their own representatives as much as they are from the present managers and owners if they do not live up to the excessive expectations fostered by ideas now in circulation—as they cannot. A degree of alienation can be detected even from the present trade unions in the very low polls in the voting for trade union office. But this abstention may be due not so much to dissatisfaction with what the trade unions

[78]

do as to the reluctance of many people to take interest in public affairs, including the organisation of their own working lives.

2. Representatives would be elected from among the 'talkers', industrial agitators and 'politicians', who believe that anything is possible and promise workers instant paradise if they are put in charge. When this paradise fails to materialise —as it must, since reality cannot be abolished—they will say that this is because they, the 'talkers', are not in full command, and thus make life for the real organisers even more difficult by incessant demands for more money and less disciplined work.

The terrain is now being prepared for such antics. An article on 'Who wants participation?', by Mr Harvie Ramsay,[1] comes out against participation in return for adopting 'responsible' attitudes by the workers since that would allegedly mean 'safeguarding profits at the workers' expense' and since decisions would be made 'by the preconditioned frame of reference, not by the worker'. Mr Ramsay, a lecturer in economics at Strathclyde University, obviously does not understand that 'the preconditioned frame of reference', i.e. the market, is determined by the wishes of all workers as consumers, and that it is not possible for anybody to work in a vacuum without taking notice of what other people want.

5. 'Democracy', Workers' Ownership and Altruism

(a) 'Industrial democracy'

When people talk about 'industrial democracy' they seem to misunderstand what 'democracy' normally means. It does not simply mean decisions taken by a majority of votes. If that were so, we could have scientific democracy, engineering democracy, and medical democracy—which is obvious nonsense. It is nonsense because democracy cannot apply where the decision primarily depends on expertise. It does not so depend when there is a clear element of choice, when there are several solutions. This happens most frequently in politics where there is choice between the programmes of various parties. That is why democracy belongs to politics and cannot be easily transposed elsewhere. Fundamentally, democracy implies the choice between goals or ends.

There cannot be any doubt about the end, the purpose, of an enterprise. It is to produce goods people want at the lowest

[1] *New Society*, 30 September, 1976.

possible price. Workers as consumers are quite clear about that: they want abundant goods at low prices. It is then pure demagogy to imply that workers as producers can democratically decide what they are going to do in their enterprise and how much they will be paid for it.

The wishes of workers for a higher standard can be satisfied only if output increases *in line with demand*. If workers put their wishes as producers first, or confound the efforts of the organisers, they frustrate themselves as consumers.

(b) Ownership by workers

It is sometimes suggested that weakness of labour management could be resolved by making workers owners of the capital. This solution might deal with the problem of responsibility, but it would hardly alter the low propensity to save. Concentration of ownership in a much smaller number of hands would follow in due course, as careful owners become separated from careless owners.

'Careless' and 'careful' may not be the correct terms: the incomes of many people are so low that it is natural for them not to save (p. 67). Unless prevented by law, they would sell their capital shares to add to their families' consumption. Others, who may indeed be called careless, would sell their shares not because of need but because they are inclined to put present before future satisfaction. The resulting concentration of ownership could be prevented only by legislation, which would take any spontaneity out of this kind of capital ownership.

Spontaneity has been widely eliminated from capital ownership through its institutionalisation by pension and insurance funds. How far can this lack of personal involvement go without impeding entrepreneurial activity to an even larger extent than has already happened? Possibly it matters less in large companies which tend to be bureaucratic and where the work is routine. What would happen to creative work which is required to start new ventures and to manage smaller, not yet firmly established, enterprises?

How would workers be made owners and how would capital shares be allotted? Would everyone receive a share in the total capital of the country as a whole or in larger enterprises? Would people who work in smaller enterprises receive no capital? Would those who happen to work in enterprises with less capital-intensive technology be given less than others? Would capital shares be distributed out of profits? If so, it would be hardly worthwhile having them: they would bear little or no income because their dividends depend on profits. And if shares were thinly spread over the whole population, ownership and responsibility attaching to them would be watered down to practically nothing. This is especially true of general workers' investment funds run by trade unions as mooted in some countries, such as Sweden or Holland.

Basque workers' co-operatives and Mr Jay

Among those who advocate workers' co-operatives and ownership is the former Economics Editor of *The Times*, Mr Peter Jay. He believes that the only available permanent solution which could reconcile high employment and collective bargaining is to convert by law all enterprises above a minimum size into workers' co-operatives.[1] As practical evidence that workers' co-operatives can cope with the realities of modern industrial life, Mr Jay described in *The Times* (7 and 14 April, 1977) a successful network of co-operatives, called Mondragon, in the Basque provinces of Spain, with about 13,000 members and £200 million turnover.

There is a sea of difference between a group of *voluntary* co-operatives and the conversion *by law* of all enterprises *above a minimum size* into co-operatives. Further there is an ocean of difference between the functioning of a system of management in a few enterprises run by highly motivated people and the application of the same system to the whole of the economy. The very successful management of the Italian National Oil Corporation (ENI) by the business tycoon Enrico Mattei does not mean that a fully nationalised economy such as the Soviet economy will work satisfactorily.

Mr Jay does not expect workers' co-operatives to be more efficient than private enterprise, since they would then have arisen spontaneously. His central argument in their favour is that co-operatives would have to sink or swim, and the workers would have to accept the market distribution and limitation of incomes. This essay has tried to show that there is very little reason to expect that this would be the result of worker-managed enterprises; the Yugoslav experience points in the

[1] Peter Jay, *A General Hypothesis of Employment, Inflation and Politics*, Occasional Paper 46, IEA, 1976.

opposite direction: that the problems would become more intractable.

The Basque co-operatives are very similar to the type of workers' enterprise discussed in this essay (p. 64). But Mr Jay objects to two of their features:

1. Workers should not invest their savings in the enterprise in which they work; it would be too risky for them to put all their eggs in the same basket. Investment elsewhere would considerably reduce workers' responsibility, which Mr Jay wants since he talks about sinking or swimming. Or would it be only a very limited responsibility? But as long as there is any responsibility, and the risk does not fall on outside capital, which it should not, it makes no difference. Any loss, or limited loss, should fall on the workers (they are the entrepreneurs). And if they do not pay it out of their savings they would have to pay it out of their wages.

2. There should be no 'bank', no external body introduced into the worker-customer relationship, because of the danger that the disregard for commercial realities would reappear if the workers could blame 'the bank' for unpalatable decisions. Undoubtedly, banks are often scapegoats for the unpleasant sides of economic life. In Yugoslavia they are under attack because they are not managed by 'direct producers' (production workers)—as though producers could manage them properly in a different way. What is resented is that banks are sometimes reluctant to advance money to cover losses, for unprofitable investment and for the stockpiling of unsaleable goods, which would suit some group of workers. Nobody seems to be entirely clear that, by allowing the funds to be used in this way, the banks lower the efficiency of the economy and reduce everybody's income.

This truth will finally have to sink in. By eliminating banks, the economy would become more inflexible. And the dissatisfaction of people who still have not grasped that they cannot get out of the economy more than they have put into it would turn against another scapegoat, presumably the government. It would be asked to subsidise enterprises that failed because they were inefficient or produced things nobody wanted, as it is sometimes in Yugoslavia.

Unfortunately, most of those who keep devising new economic systems try in essence to abolish reality. They want everyone to do whatever he likes and be given whatever he wants.

[82]

Banks and governments do not prevent us from achieving this state of bliss. What prevents us is the physical fact that all of us cannot consume more than we produce.

(c) Altruism in managing enterprises

It may be objected that the difficulties inherent in workers' management will appear only if the workers act selfishly in their own interest, but not if their actions were altruistically motivated. But this objection is not convincing. Does a worker act from altruistic motives if he acts against his individual interests and the interests of his family? Would workers act altruistically if they gave capital away instead of amassing it and transforming it into incomes for themselves? Is that supposition realistic?

To whom would they give it? To produce most efficiently capital must go where it pays best, that is, where it contributes most to the satisfaction of demand; but if workers are expected to be altruistic capital must not seek the highest return. To assure rational investment would then require some kind of state-directed central 'plan', with all the well-known consequences. The Cubans and the Chinese were trying to run their planned systems on the basis of moral appeals and incentives (to the mild amusement of the more experienced Soviet communists). The results have been such that the Cubans have switched back to economic stimulation and the Chinese seem to be about to do so. (One of the most expensive ways of 'socialist construction' in Eastern Europe was the so-called 'voluntary work'.)

The idea of an economy based on pure altruism is so outlandish that Marx never considered it could happen before the coming of perfect abundance. Then it would not be difficult to be altruistic instead of selfish, because in any event everyone would always get whatever he wanted. But abundance is not going to come tomorrow or in the next century. In the meantime Marx prescribed the adage 'To everybody according to his *work*', which almost smacks of selfishness. What is worse, *there is no direct way of measuring work except by its value in the market.* This yardstick can be easily found wanting by perfectionists but it is the only measure we have, unless we choose arbitrary political or bureaucratic decisions on what is 'just', which in practice is even more imperfect.

If any politician or trade unionist (or economist) claims that

[83]

the market and private ownership of the means of production are based on selfishness, and there is some other system based on altruism, he should, if he is serious (and honest), describe how this other system is supposed to work. Would an individual not be allowed to look after himself and his family? Would he have to look after somebody else? Whom? His neighbours? A peasant family in India? World population in general? And how could he assure himself that somebody else will in due time look after him and his family? At any rate, if he transferred his whole income to others, he would also have to be concerned that they obtained what they wanted; and this could happen only through their money-backed demand in the market.

In practice, altruism can be combined with a market capitalist system,[1] and any amount of nastiness and selfishness with any other system. The moral quality of life depends on people, not on rules: the rules can always be violated. The operation of a market presupposes a moral and legal framework. Some activities are prohibited, market or no market. These prohibitions can, of course, be flouted; but so they can under any other system. Any capitalist can put the money earned by running a successful enterprise aside and use it charitably—as many did in the 19th century: hence many of the hospitals still used by the National Health Service. The market is merely a mechanism through which people can express their wishes. Private ownership is a device to make people look after producer goods. It is a caricature to pretend it is simply a vehicle for selfishness.

The functioning of an economic system cannot be made dependent on the goodwill of individuals and groups and on exhortation. It has to be constructed in such a way that actors pursue the general good by pursuing their own interests. Adam Smith did not trust the capitalists. That is why he was so enthusiastic about the 'invisible hand' of competition.

6. CONCLUSIONS

1. Under workers' management there is no necessary connection between economic decisions and their consequences. The initial decision to organise a factory cannot be taken by the future workforce. And when it is established the

[1] *The Economics of Charity*, Readings No. 12, IEA, 1974.

composition changes so that the consequences do not necessarily fall on those who have taken the decisions.

2. If workers neither own capital nor pay full market interest rates for its borrowed use, it is in their interest to amass it and prevent it being invested where it produces most.

3. Workers as producers demand equal pay for equal skills and jobs, so that they resist variation of their incomes according to market results. This pressure flouts consumer sovereignty, not least their own interests as consumers.

4. Even if consumers' sovereignty could be preserved by strict monetary policy, there would still be no psychological-institutional mechanism which would make workers administer the factories in the general interest by running them in their own. Their propensity to save could still be too low and they could still erode the enterprise's capital.

5. Workers *en masse* cannot take decisions which require knowledge and experience plus up-to-date information. They can at best elect managers and insist that they act in their own sectional interests, i.e. pay higher wages than warranted and preserve employment at any cost.

6. Basically 'democracy' implies decisions involving the choice between several goals, which makes it difficult to apply the concept to an enterprise the essential aim of which is to produce what customers want at the lowest possible price.

7. The transfer of ownership to the workers of an enterprise by law would create a very rigid economy, especially if they were not allowed to sell their newly acquired property and use the proceeds for themselves. It would not create economic responsibility in the way that is inherent in separate ownership of capital.

8. No economic system can be based exclusively or predominantly on altruism.

9. No economic or industrial system can be perfect; the task is to choose the one that in practice is least imperfect. Nor can an economic system by itself bring happiness to the world except by providing consumer goods and services. Like patriotism, perfectionist talk about 'industrial democracy' is not enough: even worse, it can be harmful by arousing expectations that cannot be fulfilled.

[85]

10. After their experience with the abolition of the private ownership of the means of production and the introduction first of central planning and then of self-management, Yugoslav sociologists have come to the conclusion that management is a continuous power which can be disciplined by private ownership of capital. The pursuit of the long-term interests of capital owners leads them under competition to cater for workers as consumers.

PART III

Employee Participation
and
Consumer Sovereignty

The Real Lesson of Germany

JOHN B. WOOD

Of many possible reasons for the contrast between the success of the German and the failure of the British economy during the last 30 years, the German system of 'workers on boards' is of least importance, and probably irrelevant. Even the Bullock Committee does not claim much for it. At one point (Chapter 6, para. 50), the vague assertion is made that

> 'many [sic] of those we met saw a strong and direct connection between the success of the West German economy since World War II and the presence of employee representatives on supervisory boards'.

And at another point (Chapter 3, para. 13) the report resorts to innuendo. Having referred to employee respresentatives in Sweden and Germany, it comments:

> 'The fact that the West German and Swedish economies, despite differences between the social philosophies of the two countries, have been among the most successful in the world—not least in avoiding the industrial conflict which has cost Britain so dear— has not escaped notice'.

Nor should the use of *non sequiturs* and the *post hoc ergo propter hoc* fallacy escape notice. Moreover, as will appear later, the Committee's range of contacts and meetings in Germany seem to have been incomplete.

German economic success: market economy, not workers on boards

It has been the greater reliance on competitive markets, less detailed government interference in industry, the absence of nationalisation (indeed, a policy of de-nationalisation), the tight control of money supply and a disdain for vindictive taxes, which, taken together, have brought about a higher rate of growth and a lower rate of inflation in the 'social market economy' of Germany than Britain has ever dreamed of. Internationally, the German Government lends, the British Government borrows. More skilful economic management in Germany along the lines established originally by Dr Ludwig

[89]

Erhard has meant that whereas 30 years ago £1 bought 16 Deutschmark for the British tourist, now it buys just under 4.

Clearly, the labour market is likely to work more successfully in an expanding economy, and especially one in which opinion remains sharply hostile to any development that might precipitate inflation, whether apparently initiated by government or unions. Above all, Germany has been decisively helped by the wholly different role played by the trade unions, which operate within a responsible and detailed legal framework, in strong contrast to the lawlessness of British trade unions, especially since 1974.

Within the whole structure of labour law and industrial relations, schemes for worker participation form only a part, and 'workers on the board' a still smaller part. What has mattered most for the effective working of the labour market has been the small number of unions, their clearly defined legal responsibilities and the agreed limits to their activities. The main differences must be summariesd briefly to discern the real lesson to be learned from German experience.

Closed shops illegal

Unions in Germany have to be independent of any ties with a political organisation, membership is voluntary and, under the constitution, closed shops are illegal (as is the case throughout Europe except Eire and Britain). Stringent conditions and standards must be met before a union is eligible to engage in collective bargaining. Once achieved, collective agreements are legally binding on all parties—as is again the case in practically every European country except Britain. Neither unions nor their officials enjoy any special legal immunities, whereas in Britain many acts, otherwise illegal, are permitted if in pursuit of a 'trade dispute'.

Strikes are illegal unless a number of conditions are fulfilled. They must be demanded by a 75 per cent majority of the work force concerned (not just of votes cast). They are illegal if their aim is political, or if they would be in breach of a collective agreement, or if conciliation procedures have not been exhausted, or if they stop essential deliveries or services to the public. Furthermore, 'sympathy' strikes (i.e. not against one's own employer) are illegal and demarcation disputes unknown, since there are only 16 unions organised on an industry-wide basis open to all workers regardless of their professional status.

[90]

British unions virtually outside the law

From this brief summary of some of the main features of German labour law, it is at once obvious that by comparison British trade unions are virtually outside the law. It may seem surprising, therefore, that this contrast was not thought to merit any discussion in the 162 pages of the Bullock Report, despite bland claims of support for its proposals from European experience.

What is still more surprising is that these differences are completely ignored in the two special reports prepared by 'expert' academics to assess European experience on behalf of the Committee. Admittedly, in an explanation of 'parity' representation in the German coal, iron and steel industries there is a curt recognition that

'the scheme might work differently within a different framework of company and labour law'.[1]

But the proposition is not explored. How can co-determination be discussed, let alone evaluated, except within the legal and institutional framework? And yet in 'a number of visits' by 'some members of the committee' to discuss 'current arrangements with those who have had first-hand experience of them', no mention seems to have been made of the legal structure. The Committee's failure to detect these significant and conspicuous differences in labour law between Germany and Britain can perhaps best be explained by their anxiety to take 'into account in particular the proposals of the Trade Union Congress report on industrial democracy', which completely ignored them.

German 'co-determination' (Mitbestimmung)

Nevertheless, it is only within the legal framework that the whole structure of co-determination can be assessed. And would it not be sensible to review participation from the bottom upwards, rather than the other way round, since it is plainly at the lower levels of industry that worker involvement matters most to workers, as indeed German experience demonstrates?

At the root of the German system of co-determination is the

---

[1] P. L. Davies, 'European experience with worker representatives on the board', in *Industrial Democracy: European Experience*, HMSO, 1976, p. 64.

employees' council, operating in the plant. Virtually every factory has had a works council since 1920, except during the Nazi years. Its rights and duties have been defined by laws passed in 1920, 1952, and 1972, covering most matters affecting employees, except wages and salaries. Management is specifically required to discuss hours, overtime, *methods* (not amounts) of payment, hiring and firing, safety, welfare and training. Failure to consult may prove to be a breach of law. Projected mergers, re-location of plants, and the introduction of new techniques must also be discussed, and all disagreements have to be referred to a conciliation board.

A 'finance committee' of the works council is entitled to information about the company's financial progress; and in larger companies a written report cleared by this committee must be sent to all employees quarterly.

The importance of these works councils (as indeed of any committee in a plant) is precisely that their closeness at least gives the worker a chance, and perhaps even a 'feel', of participating in matters which concern him most urgently through genuine representatives whom he has not only elected, but may have met or know quite well. In contrast, 'worker directors' as proposed by Bullock, even if elected by all employees, must be remote and are unlikely to provoke a feeling of participation on the shop-floor. Again, some kind of labour representation on the German supervisory board dates back to 1920 but has become more complicated in form and method as it has spread and approaches near parity of representation, to be accomplished in 1978.

Capital and labour: equality or conflict?

Co-determination in Germany cannot be assessed unless put into this perspective of a legally imposed and institutionally buttressed 'order' for labour operating within a 'social market economy'. But even though the German system of two-tier boards is far preferable to the one proposed by Bullock, it illustrates some of the difficulties which must eventually develop because of the inherent contradiction in the assumption that capital and labour are equal and that their interests and functions are identical.

In summarising the TUC proposals, the Bullock report refers to the view 'that capital and labour are in some respects equal partners in the modern enterprise',[1]

and later to the TUC demand that

'the way in which policy is formed in an enterprise be altered to reflect *equality* between labour and capital in the running of an enterprise'.[2]

But, in the short run at least, there is a conflict of interest here which must become more acute as 'parity' of representation is approached. Labour interests will inevitably come first for worker representatives[3] who will naturally press for higher wages and salaries, better conditions and job security, in opposition to management's primary aim of serving the public most effectively by promoting profitability through efficiency and cost control. Union pressure must be towards raising costs, managements' towards lowering them.

Moreover, labour is in an entirely different situation as the co-operant factor of production, which would not be employed at all without the capital provided by shareholders. An employee's remuneration from economic activity rests on a contractual relationship, the investor's relationship is a residual one, in that he is only rewarded at all if the activity is successful and then only after all other claims have been satisfied.

If this distinction is blurred the effective working of both the labour and the capital markets is threatened. Worker directors will be able to put job security before profitability and thus reduce both occupational and geographical mobility and, of course, the creation of wealth. Investors, on the other hand, deprived of the power of dismissal which their equity gives them over the managers they have appointed to run their company, will be unable to prevent the dissipation of their money. They will either find other ways to invest, or save less. Capital will either leave the country (or not come), or be consumed as its rate of return and security are reduced.

Labour-capital alliance against the consumers

One unfortunate way in which labour and capital might resolve the conflict between them in conditions of legally imposed 'parity' on the board would be an alliance against

[1] Bullock Report, Chapter 4, para. 4.

[2] *Ibid.*, para. 6.

[3] [Compare the Yugoslav experience: Part II, *passim.*—ED.]

[93]

the consumer. Such a 'ganging up' of two producer interests would add a new dimension to Adam Smith's much quoted dictum about people of the same trade seldom meeting together without the conversation ending in a conspiracy against the public. This comment remains much more to the point than the hope expressed by the Bullock Committee 'that the effect on consumers of employee representation will be marginal' (Chapter 6, para. 4). Nor can Bullock's treatment of the interests of investors be described as other than disingenuous. The conflict goes much deeper than considerations of economic efficiency, in the sense of the better or worse use of economic resources. What is really at stake is whether investment decisions are to be left in private hands or not.

In paragraph 38 of Chapter 6 Bullock refers to submissions which

'taking the view that employee representation on boards would have a beneficial influence on the efficiency and viability of companies concluded that in the long run the interests of investors would be enhanced. Their willingness to provide capital would at worst be unaffected, and at best increased, leading to a positive desire to invest in companies with the new board structure, and to a wish on the part of the overseas investors to expand their operations in this country to take advantage of the improved industrial relations'.

The Report then continues:

'Such a view was implicit in the remarks made to us during our visit to Germany, by the Federal Chancellor, Dr Helmut Schmidt, among others, who expressed belief that the implementation of employee representation on company boards would have a positive influence on the whole British economy and would not be inimical to foreign investment in the United Kingdom.'

One wonders whether the Federal Chancellor (or overseas investors) would have been of the same opinion had they been able to read the article by Paul Davies which appeared in the *New Statesman* on 18 February, 1977, in which the majority report was described as

'a highly intelligent and sophisticated contribution to the debate on the *socialisation of private capital*'. (My italics.)

Mr Davies was one of the Bullock Committee's expert assesssors of European experience.

* * *

[94]

In all these ways co-determination in the sense of stronger or equal representation of labour on the board not only threatens the best use of resources, but may lead to a concentration of economic power. It also has other dangers. One concerns monopoly law. Suppose that the 'worker directors' in Company 'Y' belong to the same union as those nominated to the board of its principal competitor, Company 'Z'. Suppression of competition would become easier. But if there were to be a contravention of monopoly law then the ordinary directors might be prosecuted, while under Bullock the employee directors could not be!

A further consequence is as neglected as it is important. The introduction of worker directors throughout industry must mean the development of alternative career structures in business life. There would be two ways to the top, one via management, the other via the unions. Since there is far more potential managerial talent off the shop floor, to offer equal or near-equal representation is, of course, discriminatory, and the results must be wasteful.

Overseas experience unhelpful

In the end the experience of other countries is of little help. As Mr Eric Batstone remarks at the beginning of his review:[1]

'The introduction of worker directors is so recent in many countries that no reliable data on their actual performance are available'.

Even German experience offers little guidance. The origins of what is now taken to be a system for employee representation were in fact legislation to strengthen *shareholders'* control over companies in the last century, re-shaped by the 1945 occupying powers' notion of 'safeguarding' German heavy industries against possible re-nazification by the presence of employees on boards.

Essentially, however, the German system has caused little trouble partly because employees will still have only minority representation even after the implementation of the 1976 Act. More importantly, both the legal structure and the prevailing ideology are quite different, and encourage the full pursuit of the company's interests. The tendency for management and

---

[1] 'Industrial democracy and worker representation at board level: a review of the European experience', in *Industrial Democracy: European Experience*, HMSO, 1976. Mr Batstone is Research Fellow at the SSRC Industrial Relations Research Unit, University of Warwick.

worker directors to conspire to promote the efficiency of their factory is derided even in Germany as 'company egoism'.

This community of interest hardly exists in Britain, where many unions are pledged to destroy the market system. As long as the TUC itself is fully committed to the principle of public ownership conflicts are bound to arise. Even more important than the differences in legal framework between Britain and Germany is the widespread acceptance by politicians, the media and the public in Germany of an economy based on private enterprise and competitive markets. If this ideological climate were to change, as some observers fear is already beginning, then worker participation would convert German industry into a battleground of debilitating economic conflict, as the Bullock majority report seems intent to do in British industry.

Bullock's Basic Blunder

Producers and Consumers:
Collusion or Confrontation?

RALPH HARRIS

The generally hostile reception given to the majority report of the Bullock Committee suggests it may prove the last manifestation of a school of thought that has risen to dominance over the very period of Britain's relative economic decline since the 1880s. This watershed also marked the emergence of the Fabians with the aim of transforming the free society by permeating the thinking of the Liberal, Conservative and (later) Labour parties. Almost 100 years later, they have gone far towards their goal. Their success may be summarised as lending intellectual respectability to far-reaching proposals for ever more ingenious ways of dissipating the fruits of prosperity based on consumer sovereignty in the market without equal thought about the effects of weakening the market in the future. The Bullock Committee's proposal to subject competitive enterprise to a dominant producer interest would carry this myopic zeal to its logical, most damaging, conclusion.

Source of prosperity?

Britain's economic decline was not inevitable. Apologists for our poor relative performance have differed in variously blaming the effects of two world wars, the absence of raw materials, our limited home market, the costs of empire (or alternatively of its liquidation), our dependence on foreign trade. None of these factors is sufficient to explain Britain's failure. The enviable achievements of Germany, France, Belgium, Holland and even Switzerland have been won mostly in the face of similar if not identical handicaps. Contemporary evidence confirms the lesson of history, that economic progress does not chiefly depend on physical circumstances, nor on the abundance of specific, indigenous material resources, not even domestic supplies of land, fuel, food, capital, all of which can be made good through foreign trade, as the example of Hong Kong vividly demonstrates.

The chief source of economic progress is compounded of

energy plus enterprise in adapting the arts of production and distribution to supply the changing goods and services demanded at home or abroad. But plainly energy and enterprise are not sufficient. There was plenty of both *beneath the surface* in Germany before Erhard wrought his economic miracle, or in India today, or even in Russia since the revolution. To bring these human qualities into effective operation they must be animated and harnessed. They require an economic and social environment that both galvanises and guides individual efforts towards the creation of wealth. It was the achievement of 18th-century British thinkers to conceive and of 19th-century British statesmen to pioneer a framework of laws for a market economy which, for all its imperfections, made possible improvements in standards of living unknown in any earlier country or epoch. This mechanism has been weakened enough by government; it would be further debilitated—perhaps fatally—by Bullock.

Capitalism versus capitalists?

The appropriate legal and institutional environment does not depend on simply establishing private ownership of the material means of production, as is naïvely supposed by Marxist critics and some conservative defenders of 'free enterprise'. The self-interest of producers does not automatically coincide with the best interests of their customers. The interest of producers is in securing maximum return from their products at the highest price they can extract from the customer. None of this was strange to the great philosopher of liberal capitalism, Adam Smith, who penned the most damning brief indictment of an economy dominated by producer interests:

> 'People of the same trade seldom meet together, even for merriment and diversion, but the conversation ends in a conspiracy against the public, or in some contrivance to raise prices.'[1]

The key to understanding the fallacy in the Bullock report is that, although workers and capitalists may differ over the respective shares of wages and profits, as joint producers they have a *common* interest in maximising the surplus of revenue over costs of production. Indeed, since the essential ingredients for economic progress identified above as human energy and

---

[1] *The Wealth of Nations,* ed. Edwin Cannan, Vol. I, Ch. X, Pt. II, Methuen, 1950 (6th edn.), p. 144.

enterprise can be roughly equated with worker and capitalist, we might today re-write Smith's warning to include: 'People of the same *trade union . . .*'

Necessity of competition

This potential conflict between the interests of producers and consumers runs wider than the wish of capitalists (and their workers) for high prices (and wages) and of the customers for low prices. Producers who have committed their capital and skills to an industry have a powerful motive to restrict the entry of new products or methods of production; their customers have the opposite interest in welcoming more efficient techniques. Since economic progress depends on making resources go furthest by encouraging the replacement of less productive by more productive methods, this conflict goes to the centre of the Bullock debate on the management of productive enterprise.

The conundrum that economists have to solve can therefore be formulated as two apparently irreconcilable propositions: first, private enterprise and effort are the most powerful engine of economic progress; and second, producers—both capitalists and labour—are naturally inclined to advance their own interest at the expense of their customers. How then can we harmonise these powerful private interests with long-run public prosperity? The answer has been provided by a long line of classical economists from Smith and Hume through Mill, Marshall and Knight to Robbins, Hayek and Friedman, who have refined the philosopher's stone that transmutes the drive to maximise profits and wages into the public advantage. The solution was to convert *private* into *competitive* enterprise.

Consumer sovereignty

Economic progress thus depends on setting human energies and enterprise free within an environment of competition that maintains active tension in the continuing tug-of-war between the producer and consumer interests; between the forces making for high prices (profits, wages) from *established* sources of production and those making for maximum efficiency from *all possible* (including foreign) sources.

A competitive market does not emerge from *laissez-faire*. It is the outcome of a deliberately contrived legal and institutional framework that includes the definition of property rights,

[99]

the critical importance of which is analysed by Chiplin and Coyne in Part I. When they say 'Rewards and penalties are the prime movers in human endeavour', they succinctly express the creative role of effort and enterprise operating in a competitive framework that enables producers to prosper only so long as they give consumers better value than alternative suppliers. In effect, capitalist and worker are given freedom to sell their joint product at the highest price they can get, so long as they accept the discipline of competition which elevates the consumer into ultimate authority. When Adam Smith declared 'Consumption is the sole end and purpose of all production', he concluded 'the interest of the producer ought to be attended to, only so far as it is necessary for promoting that of the consumer'.

On the foundation of this central proposition, market economists have constructed an elaborate analysis which establishes the general presumption that efficiency, economic freedom and 'just distribution' are best served by the impersonal interaction of competitive supply and consumer choice in open markets. Against all practicable alternatives, this conception upholds the valuations of rewards for capital and labour established impartially in competitive markets as the nearest approximation to 'social justice'. Competition, moreover, brings the unique political advantage of minimising coercion; it replaces conflict of interest by co-operation based on the mutual gains from trade between willing buyers and sellers.

The perennial danger to this harmonious outcome springs from the heavier concentration and narrower focus of producers than of consumers. Not only are producers more easily brought together; they have a larger stake in a particular product than consumers whose spending is fragmented between a large number of purchases. Whilst every producer supports competition in the materials he buys, each would prefer to monopolise the product he sells. While workers naturally welcome many outlets for their skills, they would prefer firms for which they work to enjoy a monopoly in selling their products. The most immediate interest of workers is, furthermore, vested narrowly in preserving existing employment and methods against the challenge of competition. And this proclivity British trade unions have amply demonstrated, especially since monetary inflation and new laws have compounded their market power.

The blunder of the Bullock majority was to ignore the threat to the consumer of further entrenching the producer interest by allying unions and managements in the 'conspiracy against the public' of which Smith warned 200 years ago.

The logic—and illogic—of Luddism

Economic progress depends on the ease with which new products and improved methods of production can make their way against the *status quo*. The lasting benefit is reaped by the generality of consumers whilst the transitional disturbance is felt by producers who stand to lose their investments in equipment or skills. The equity investor cannot justifiably complain when his capital is put at risk in this way. But before the days of unemployment insurance, redundancy payments, and tax refunds, the employee faced a more pressing hardship.

It is, therefore, not surprising that in the face of the long-run improvements in 19th-century industry, workers reacted to short-term dislocations of employment in a negative, restrictive and even destructive way. The story of Ned Ludd's attack on weaving machines in 1799 is better known than the more violent episodes of displaced hand-workers burning factories and assaulting employers and even inventors like Kay of flying shuttle fame. Their subjective logic can be understood; yet if every sectional producer interest had been able to frustrate change in working conditions, not only would the consumers have been denied the benefits of modern industry, but the workers would have lost the chance of better-paid and less onerous employments. If the industrial revolution prevailed against such violent resistance, a principal reason must have been the speedy demonstration of the objective economic logic that the new labour-saving machines reduced costs, enlarged markets and multiplied jobs. Dramatic proof came earliest in cotton textiles where between 1820 and 1840 employment increased from around 50,000 to nearer 500,000. Yet if unions had been as powerful in the 1820s as they are today, this beneficial shift of capital and labour into new industries— which marks all economic development—would have been delayed to the lasting cost of producers no less than consumers.

The development of trade union law is a matter of utmost complexity, as shown by continued controversy about its application to cases that have come before the courts up to modern times. What is clear is that between the Combination

Acts of 1799 and 1800 and the Trade Disputes Act of 1906 the legal status of trade unions changed from being illegal conspiracies to enjoying, in Dicey's words,

'a privilege and protection not possessed by any other person or body of persons, whether corporate or unincorporate, throughout the United Kingdom'.[1]

This reversal of law from 'unjust severity' to 'unjust favouritism', which has gone much further by 1977, was due partly to the sentiment that trade unions represented the 'underdog', but increasingly to the electoral power exerted through the widening franchise by the Labour Party as the political instrument of the trade unions. Their powers and immunities in pursuit of anything that passes as a 'trade dispute'—however trivial—have reached the stage where, in the literal sense, they are legally *irresponsible* in the deployment of monopoly pressures against employers, consumers and even governments. The logical pretext for such favours was to redress the balance between 'master' and 'servant'; the illogical outcome has been to buttress the sectional producer-interest of workers in resisting changes in production—in transport, steel, newspapers, shipbuilding, mining, docks, airways, plastics and paper—of overwhelming long-run benefit to consumers and society.

British disease—1897 . . .

The relative decline of British industry dates back to the closing decades of the 19th century when, in private correspondence with the Master of Balliol,[2] Alfred Marshall described 'the crisis of our industry':

'For the last twenty years we have indeed been still progressing; but we have been retrograding relatively to the Americans and to the nations of central Europe . . .'

His reasons are particularly significant because he combined exact observation of industrial developments with sympathy for working-class aspirations in the co-operative and trade union movements. Yet, in the same letter (written in 1897), he described as an 'unmixed evil' and 'a threat to national well-being':

'. . . the dominance in some unions of the desire to "make work", and an increase in their power to do so'.

[1] *Law and Public Opinion in England,* Macmillan, 2nd edn., 1914, p. xlvi.
[2] A. C. Pigou (ed.), *Memorials of Alfred Marshall,* Macmillan, 1925, p. 399.

He characterised ruling union minorities as 'wanting to compel others to put as little work as possible into the hour'. As an example, he cited the bricklayers' unions:

'If [they] could have been completely destroyed twenty years ago, I believe bricklayers would now be as well off and more self-respecting . . . and cottages would be 10 per cent or 20 per cent larger all round. And, meanwhile, healthier bricklayers' TU's would have grown up.'

In making locomotives, Marshall estimated: '3 Glasgow men are needed to do the work of 1 American'. He sadly condemned the Amalgamated Society of Engineers for likewise insisting on over-manning of machines. Arguing that the union's victory in the strike (which prompted his correspondence) would threaten 'a lasting check' to 'the progress upwards of the English working classes', Marshall concluded:

'If the men should win, and I were an engineering employer, I would sell my works for anything I could get and emigrate to America'.[1]

In a revealing correspondence with the Bishop of Durham,[2] Marshall identified the more fundamental source of malaise as misconceived criticisms of competition, particularly by the Christian Socialists, which:

'. . . since 1860 have done so much to undermine the vigour and honest work of English industry, and have removed her from the honourable leadership which she used to hold among the nations . . .'

Since Marshall's time, this process has been carried much further. In pursuit of the phantom of economic security, public policy, invariably prompted by producer-interests, has sought to shelter established industries, regions, firms, employments against competition from more up-to-date techniques.[3] The last 100 years has witnessed a decline in the common law presumption against 'restraint of trade' and the rise of open and disguised protectionism in the forms of tariffs, imperial preference, marketing boards, regional policy, 'rationalisation',

---

[1] In this passage Marshall anticipated the analysis of Professor W. H. Hutt that union power discourages investment and reduces the improvement in real wages. (*The Theory of Collective Bargaining, 1930-1975*, Hobart Paperback 8, IEA, 1975.)

[2] *Memorials*, pp. 391-5.

[3] A fuller analysis will be found in Professor G. C. Allen's *The British Disease*, Hobart Paper 67, IEA, 1976.

licensing or prohibition of new competitors, subsidies and government contracts to failing industries, national planning and outright nationalisation.

Instead of easing the shift of capital and labour from declining to expanding employments, both Labour and Conservative governments have yielded to short-term electoral calculations by bolstering the *status quo*.[1] Even since the Second World War, when extensive welfare arrangements were available to cushion the impact of change, the guiding expedient for policy has been defensive and protectionist, whatever the political rhetoric about 'growth' and 'modernisation'. It may be objected that managements have often welcomed such protectionism as ardently as the unions; but when firms are prevented from innovating by labour restrictions, they have often abandoned the unequal struggle and settled for a quiet life with more or less guaranteed profits.

Confrontation—1977?

The monopoly power of trade unions to obstruct economic progress has been rendered even more damaging by the over-riding priority post-war governments gave to 'full employment' defined and pursued in a way that accelerated inflation. It is a matter of elementary economic analysis that no monopolist can dictate both the price at which he will offer his product or service and the amount he will sell. Since demand is elastic over some range, it follows that if the price is pushed too high customers will buy less. This truism applies no less to trade unions as monopoly suppliers of labour, despite their power to conscript members through the closed shop and to prohibit 'blacklegging' through coercive picketing.

Even coal miners or electricity power workers cannot increase their wage costs indefinitely without inviting unemployment as marginal customers reduce consumption or turn to alternative sources of heat—and even of light. The corrective of unemployment—the effect of a reduction in demand faced by any monopolist—applies more quickly for most workers who produce goods and services that have closer substitutes. But if government stands ready in the name of 'full employment' to expand monetary demand so as to mop up unemployment resulting from wage costs that are excessive *in relation to real*

[1] In G. C. Allen's words: '. . . the chief effect of the government's intervention between the wars was to defend the failures rather than to encourage the enterprising'. (*Ibid.*, p. 52.)

output, there is no limit to the over-pricing of labour and the resulting inflation. And as unions see through the 'money illusion' and build inflationary expectations into their wage demands, the stage is set for eventually explosive inflation.

'Producer sovereignty'

It was precisely this dilemma that led Mr Peter Jay in his Wincott Lecture[1] to float the idea of reconstructing industry on the basis of labour-run co-operatives within a market framework that would discourage worker-entrepreneurs from pricing themselves out of jobs. The theoretical ingenuity of this effort to out-flank labour monopolies by out-Bullocking the Bullock majority and making workers directly responsible for meeting their own wage bill, encounters a number of difficulties arising from the well-established conflicts between syndicalist objectives and the entrepreneurial imperatives of an economy subject to unpredictable change and uncertainty.[2] But its political defect is surely decisive: it is a scheme inspired by the wish to avoid a frontal assault on trade union monopoly, yet its implementation must arouse resistance from the controllers of trade unions who would have no place in a world of freely competing co-operative enterprises. They would accept Mr Jay's producer control but not the 'consumer sovereignty' on which he says it must rest and without which the outcome can be only a corporate state, stagnation and impoverishment.

Since he acknowledges, without attempting to resolve, what he calls 'a thousand and one very loose ends'—about ownership, labour turnover, contraction and liquidation—a more modest experiment in workers' control would be to convert the coal mines and power stations into local co-operatives that compete with one another in an open market permitting unhindered entry for new producers.

Whatever doubts may be voiced about the feasibility of Mr Jay's prescription, his rigorous diagnosis indicates that the monopoly power of trade unions poses at best a choice between mounting inflation and increasing unemployment, and at

[1] *A General Hypothesis of Employment, Inflation and Politics,* Occasional Paper 46, IEA, 1976.

[2] In their *Constitution for the Socialist Commonwealth of Great Britain,* Longmans, 1920, the Webbs admitted: '. . . a Democracy of Producers, whether it be of manual workers or of brain workers, is by the very nature of its membership perpetually tempted to seek to maintain existing processes unchanged, to discourage innovations that would introduce new kinds of labour . . .'.

worst a combination of both that must eventually disrupt our economy and polity. Against this background, it is fanciful for Bullock's partisan political theorists to expect dedication to the long-run consumer interest in progress, efficiency and mobility from union monopolies which, in Britain, have come to be guided by the short-term sectional interests of their members as producers, and have been given irresponsible power to impose those interests by strikes in breach of contract reinforced by 'blacking', picketing, psychological pressure, intimidation and immunity from actions for damages. As the surprisingly spirited evidence of the National Consumer Council emphasised, the TUC submission—which the Bullock Committee were instructed to treat as holy writ—did not even mention the consumer.

Open-market competition

The fundamental analysis shows that all who derive income from industry are victims of the schizophrenic conflict between their interests as producers—in stability, comfort, continuity, security—and as consumers—in choice, cheapness, change and other fruits of progress. No better way consistent with Western values has yet been proposed to resolve this conflict than to expose all producers to maximum competition in open markets. So long as trade unions insist on overmanning and under-mining more efficient methods of production, their members must pay the price in lower real wages and diminished prospects of more rewarding employment.

The exercise of monopoly power by union representatives on company boards must discourage productive investment. As Henry Simons demonstrated in his seminal 'Reflections on Syndicalism',[1] it is vain for Mr Michael Foot or Mr James Prior to expect unions to refrain from exerting their power because 'monopoly . . . has no use save abuse'. In Britain in 1977 we must be approaching a confrontation with the too-long evaded reality that monopoly unions are in conflict with the broad interests of consumers and even with the longer-term interests of their own members. The solution is not along the Bullock road of even more union power. The only lasting antidote to monopoly—in labour or enterprise—is exposure to maximum competition.

[1] Reproduced in *Economic Policy for a Free Society*, University of Chicago Press, Chicago, 1948.

QUESTIONS FOR DISCUSSION

1. What light does the developing theory of property rights throw on the economics of employee representation on boards of companies?

2. If employees have a claim to representation on boards on the ground that their interests are affected by board decisions, how far have suppliers of raw materials and purchasers of the products comparable claims?

3. Why has industrial enterprise developed by capital hiring labour rather than labour hiring capital?

4. How far should ownership be linked with control and risk-taking in industrial enterprise?

5. What are the economic consequences of employees on boards representing trade unions rather than the work-force of each firm?

6. How far does 'industrial democracy' compare and contrast with political democracy?

7. How would employee representatives resolve the conflict between maximising immediate pay and optimising long-term investment?

8. How would employee representatives on boards resolve the conflict between their interest as employees and their interest as consumers?

9. Does 'worker participation' in Germany strengthen or weaken the economic case for 'worker participation' in Britain?

10. What are the lessons from Yugoslavia on the economic consequences of employee control in industrial enterprise?

FURTHER READING

(This bibliography amplifies the sources in the text.)

Alchian, Armen, and Demsetz, Harold, 'Production, Information Costs and Economic Organisation', *American Economic Review*, December 1972.

Allen, G. C., *The British Disease*, Hobart Paper 67, Institute of Economic Affairs, 1976.

Batstone, Eric, 'Industrial democracy and worker representation at board level: a review of the European experience', in *Industrial Democracy: European Experience*, HMSO, London, 1976.

Benson, Leslie, 'Market Socialism and Class Structure: Manual Workers and Managerial Power in the Yugoslav Enterprise', in Frank Parkin (ed.), *The Social Analysis of Class Structure*, Tavistock, London, 1974.

Blumberg, Paul, *Industrial Democracy, The Sociology of Participation*, Constable, London, 1968.

Clegg, Hugh, *A New Approach to Industrial Democracy*, Basil Blackwell, Oxford, 1960.

Coase, R. H., 'The Nature of the Firm', *Economica*, 1937.

Coates, K., and Topham, T., *Industrial Democracy in Great Britain*, MacGibbon & Kee, London, 1968.

Crew, Michael A., *The Theory of the Firm*, Longmans, London, 1975.

Davies, P. L., 'European experience with worker representatives on the board', in *Industrial Democracy: European Experience*, HMSO, London, 1976.

Demsetz, Harold, 'Towards a Theory of Property Rights', *American Economic Review, Papers and Proceedings*, May 1967.

Fox, Alan, *Industrial Sociology and Industrial Relations*, Research Paper No. 3, Royal Commission on Trade Unions and Employers' Associations, HMSO, London, 1966.

Furubotn, E. G., and Pejovich, Svetozar, 'Property Rights, Economic Decentralisation, and the Evolution of the Yugoslav Firm, 1965-72', *Journal of Law and Economics*, October 1973.

Hindley, Brian, 'Separation of Ownership and Control in the Modern Corporation', *Journal of Law and Economics*, April 1970.

Hutt, W. H., *The Theory of Collective Bargaining 1930-1975*, Hobart Paperback No. 8, Institute of Economic Affairs, 1975 (2nd Impression, 1977).

Jay, Peter, *A General Hypothesis of Employment, Inflation and Politics*, Sixth Wincott Memorial Lecture, Occasional Paper 46, Institute of Economic Affairs, 1976.

Meade, J. E., 'The Theory of Labour-Managed Firms and of Profit Sharing', *Economic Journal*, March 1972.

Mill, J. S., *Principles of Political Economy* (1871), University of Toronto Press, Toronto, 1965, especially Book IV, Chapter VII.

Simons, Henry, *Economic Policy for a Free Society*, University of Chicago Press, Chicago, 1948.

Sorge, Arndt, 'The Evolution of Industrial Democracy in the Countries of the European Community', *British Journal of Industrial Relations*, November 1976.

Stephens, F. H., 'Yugoslav Self Management 1945-74', *Industrial Relations Journal*, Winter 1976-77.

Stigler, G. J., 'The Xistence of x-efficiency', *American Economic Review*, March 1976.

Vanek, J., *The General Theory of Labour-Managed Market Economies*, Cornell University Press, Ithaca, N.Y., 1975.

Ward, Benjamin, 'The Firm in Illyria: Market Syndicalism', *American Economic Review*, Vol. 48, No. 4, 1958.

Webb, Sidney and Beatrice, *Industrial Democracy*, Longman, Green, London, 1897.

Report of the Committee of Inquiry on Industrial Democracy (Bullock Report), Cmnd. 6706, HMSO, London, 1977.

SOME IEA PAPERS ON INDUSTRY, MANAGEMENT AND LABOUR

Hobart Paper 67

The British Disease

A short essay on the nature and causes of the nation's lagging wealth

G. C. ALLEN

1976 £1·00

'G. C. Allen . . . deals with the cult of the amateur, the short-comings of the civil service, the absence of adequate reward for success, the low status accorded to business success. It is by no means necessary to agree with all he says to find this worthwhile reading.'

Patrick Hutber, *Sunday Telegraph*

'. . . a solid case . . . leaden with footnotes, and what is especially nasty is that the chickens that are coming home to roost now in the headlines have been crackled-over for at least a century.'

Jon Akass, *Sun*

Occasional Paper 46

Employment, Inflation and Politics

Sixth Wincott Memorial Lecture

PETER JAY

1976 60p

'It is always a delight to read pellucid prose particularly when one is led by rigid inexorability of argument to an inevitable conclusion.'

David Malbert, *Evening Standard*

[110]

Hobart Paper 58

The Price of Prosperity

Lessons from Japan

CHIAKI NISHIYAMA, G. C. ALLEN

1974   60p

'It is brief, dense and stimulating. An incisive, short paper by Professor Nishiyama is followed by a somewhat longer one by Professor G. C. Allen. The first pinpoints some of the keys to Japan's spectacular growth. The second discusses its deeper causes and attempts to draw some lessons for Britain and, by implication, for the West as a whole.'

International Affairs

'In a concise, useful and provocative *Hobart* excursion outside Britain, Nishiyama defends the "indisputable" benefits of growth. Its mainspring was a combination of the *Ringisho* system ("group dynamics *a la Japonaise*") and an orthodox monetary policy which managed to encourage both investment and competition. Professor Allen comments on these, outlines other factors (American aid, labour supply and attitudes, low defence outlays) and adds a one-page prologue on the oil crisis. There is plenty to discuss here, including possible lessons for Britain, even if of dubious practicality in the existing socio-political climate.'

W. J. Macpherson, *Economic Journal*

The Way of Enterprise

A study of the origins, problems and achievements in the growth of post-war British firms

HARRY MILLER

1963   xii + 272 pp.   £1·00

Key Discussion Book 9

Industrial Structure

An exposition of the role of industry in advanced economies. The author discusses advertising, concentration, innovation, technology and competition.

P. S. JOHNSON

1970   35p